## Praise for *Spirit in Action*

"For thousands of years, cultures around the world have explored the almost unlimited possibilities of expanding one's awareness through sacred music and dance. In her book, *Spirit in Action,* Irene Lamberti brings readers clear and concise instructions for raising our consciousness through balance, movement, and various postures. This is a great book that not only offers readers a wealth of information and wisdom teachings from a wide variety of sources, but is sure to become a classic guide for those of us who want to transcend words both in our prayers and in the expression of our joy."

—RABBI DAVID A. COOPER
Author of *God Is a Verb*

# SPIRIT IN ACTION

## Moving Meditations for Peace, Insight, and Personal Power

Irene Lamberti, D.C.

with W. Bradford DeLong, M.D.

BALLANTINE WELLSPRING™
THE BALLANTINE PUBLISHING GROUP • NEW YORK

A Ballantine Wellspring™ Book
Published by The Ballantine Publishing Group
Copyright © 2000 by Irene Lamberti, D.C.

Grateful acknowledgment is made to the following for permission to reprint
previously published material:
*Harmony Books, a division of Random House, Inc.:* excerpt from *Love Poems of Rumi* by
Deepak Chopra. Copyright © 1998 by Deepak Chopra. Reprinted by permission of
Harmony Books, a division of Random House, Inc.
*HarperCollins Publishers, Inc.:* eight prayers from *Prayers of the Cosmos: Meditations on the
Aramaic Words of Jesus* by Neil Douglas-Klotz. Copyright © 1990 by Neil Douglas-Klotz.
Reprinted by permission of HarperCollins Publishers, Inc.

www.randomhouse.com/BB/

Library of Congress Catalog Card Number: 00-102760

ISBN 0-345-43482-X

Text design by Holly Johnson

Cover photo by Andres Rentsch

Manufactured in the United States of America

First Edition: June 2000

10   9   8   7   6   5   4   3   2   1

On our lifelong spiritual journey, we each encounter hundreds of teachers and guides who influence us deeply, some directly, others as anonymous contributors to our unfolding. They may be friends, family, patients, caregivers, co-workers, or simply people we encounter by chance for a few fleeting seconds. Often they are the writers and lecturers who open up a place in our souls. They write the books that make us say, "Yes! That is what I know to be true—I just couldn't find the words to express it. Thank you for helping me define my truth."

Writers such as Larry Dossey, Marianne Williamson, Neale Donald Walsch, Daniel Quinn, Neil Douglas-Klotz, Matthew Fox, Sanaya Roman, and Marion Zimmer-Bradley use their genius to make us feel like close friends on a shared spiritual adventure, but this short list leaves out hundreds of other potent advocates of expansion and awareness to whom I am grateful. This dedication goes to all those who have had the courage and discipline to speak their truth, present their highest visions, and expand the field of possibilities for spiritual commitment.

# CONTENTS

❦

# AUTHOR'S NOTE

Throughout my adult life I have experienced God as Spirit without gender. Jewish mystics often refer to God as *Ein Sof*, which means "endlessness." In his book *God Is a Verb*, Rabbi David Cooper says:

> God is not what we think It is. God is not a thing, a being, a noun. It does not exist as existence is defined, for it takes up no space and is not bound by time. . . . *Ein Sof* should never be conceptualized in any way. It should not be called Almighty, Father, Mother, Infinite, The One, Brahma, Buddhamind, Allah, Adonoy, Elohim, El, or Shaddai; and It should never, never be called He. It is none of these names and It has no gender.

Western culture and language, however, have persistently referred to God using masculine pronouns, which distances our experience of the inclusive nature of the Unifying force (God force) of the Universe.

The purpose of this book is to offer a practice that enhances our relationship with the sacred nature of life. As this book will be released in the year 2000 C.E., I believe it is time to reject the linguistic custom of implying that God is a He. Throughout this book I refer to the concept of God in inclusive language. I offer terms such as *Spirit, the Great Mystery, the Great Unity, the Divine*, along with the pronoun *It*, as the larger context for the "Great Abstraction." In so doing, it is my intention to broaden our understanding and to offer women as well as men a linguistic model that welcomes them into the process of spiritual awakening.

# ACKNOWLEDGMENTS

A book rarely comes together without input, support, and feedback from a number of persons. This book is also a result of many hands and ideas. Most important, I wish to thank my husband, Brad DeLong, M.D., without whose partnership I would not have begun this book. His tireless thought, editing, and research brought many elements of intellectual honesty and grace to this work. His patience and love add untold joy on this journey.

My gratitude also goes to Leslie Meredith at Ballantine Wellspring, who invited me to write this book. It was her vision to bring embodied prayer to readers. She has demonstrated unswerving wisdom in her editorial directions and enthusiasm for the subject. Sage editorial commentary and suggestions from Howard Kaplan also added grace and cohesion to the form of this work.

Heartfelt thanks to Maureen Millen, CEO of IWV Media, executive producer and syndicator extraordinaire, whose faithful perseverance placed *The Aerobic Prayer* series on national television. Without her initial vision and interest in my work, the success of the television series and the interest in this book would not have happened.

To my friends Phyllis Freidman, Nancy Berkheiser, M.D., Jim Haney, and George McLaird, who read early versions of the manuscript, offering input and compassionate critique, I also offer my heartfelt gratitude. My thanks to talented photographer Marc LaMoreaux, whose professionalism made our shoots of the exercises and moving meditations a joy.

# Part I

# MOVEMENT IS SPIRIT

*The next time you look in the mirror, just look at the way the ears rest next to the head; look at the way the hairline grows; think of all the little bones in your wrist. It is a miracle. And the dance is a celebration of that miracle.*
—MARTHA GRAHAM, MODERN DANCE PIONEER AND
CHOREOGRAPHER (1894–1991)

The body is a miracle. It expresses our personal spark from the Spirit within us and surrounding us. It is our vehicle of communication with each other, with our past, our present, and—if we pay attention to it and listen to the body's messages—our future. Our body tells us who we are as no mirror can. And it can lead us into feelings of ecstasy and unity, of union with other people and with a greater Spirit.

In Western religions communicating with Spirit usually entails a mental attitude or activity. Aside from clasping our hands in prayer or genuflecting or bowing our heads in humility, we don't typically use the body in spiritual practice. Many in our culture view the body as a mere container for thought and soul and, as such, regard it as something to be maintained out of necessity. Thomas Alva Edison, for instance, said that the body was just a vehicle for the brain. These views of the body as separate from mind and spirit have produced deep emotional wounds and left many feeling alienated, ill at ease with their bodies and within themselves.

Most of us take our minds to work, our bodies to the gym, and the spirit to its own workout, for an hour or two, on the weekend. This inconsistency is symptomatic of beings that are out of balance. Mind, body, and spirit are connected; yet we have few actual practices in which all three work together to celebrate that connection. Through conscious, physical movement, however, we can learn to unite body, mind, and spirit and, further, to develop the spiritual principles of grace, endurance, and strength that can help us move forward in our life's journey. Moving our bodies provides Spirit with an important avenue into our hearts.

The form of "spirit in action" taught in this book is physical movement combined with a mindful prayer. These spiritual, physical routines will help heal any mind-body split, help you discover the innate grace and power of your own body, and give you peace of mind.

## MOVING TO REUNITE BODY AND SELF

Human beings were made to move and grow. Spirit is always present. I believe that when we keep our energy bottled up inside, or don't act in our own best interests or don't express our creative imaginings, it is Spirit's promptings that make us feel vaguely uncomfortable. Some of us are tied up in emotional and physical knots, while others are constrained by "nots," whether from our upbringing or our cultural conditioning. When our bones and joints become stiff and frozen, so, often, do our attitudes and perceptions. Using movement as part of spiritual practice opens up and stretches our body-mind so that new energy, vitality, and spirit can enter and dwell in and animate us. Mind-body prayer encourages you to breathe in the gift of life, expand your connections, and grow in personal power.

We in the West are now beginning to accept that the body can be a vehicle for spiritual expression and attainment. The practices of yoga, tai chi, martial arts, and qi gong have helped us experience the reality of the mind-body-spirit connection, as has the study of bodily energy systems such as the chakras and energy meridians in the health disciplines of Reiki, acupressure and acupuncture, reflexology, and others. Along with these practices has flourished a renaissance in spiritual rituals, tribal dance arts, and traditional church service dance. My own experiences with spirit in action in these old and new practices led me to develop the mind-body prayers, or embodied prayers, in this book.

*Spirit in Action* is a call to experience prayer as more than just an intellectual activity. It is a contemporary program that has its roots in ancient, traditional rituals. I've based the movements you'll learn in this book on those I have found in sacred dances as well as on common physical expressions of inner emotions culled from different world cultures. These prayers are acted out through a sequence of motions, just as the sentences of literal prayers are constructed from a series of words. Bodily gestures are infused with spiritual significance, creating a meaningful moving practice. When we pray with our bodies as well as our minds, we are manifesting the energy of a greater Spirit in our material plane. We invite the presence of the Creator into our everyday lives so that Its energy animates all that we do and think.

Even though our spiritual teachers have been telling us for years to recognize the interconnectedness of body, mind, and spirit, most practices actually subjugate or restrict the body. The relatively new consciousness of the past twenty years of the need for physical fitness may be just what our culture needed to nudge us into a true integration of body, mind, and spirit. Dance is one practice that can help us achieve this unity, especially dances that have been practiced for hundreds of years. Our ancestors understood the importance of facilitating the communication between the mind-body and spirit.

It dawned on me several years ago that these moving prayers were actually a very good aerobic workout. What a bonus! After that, I concentrated on developing movements that are natural for the body and not demanding on the joints, using my twenty years of experience as a practicing chiropractor, with a specialty in rehabilitative exercise.

When I began to teach and share my moving prayers with other people, even those who claimed to hate exercise told me that they loved this activity, saying, "It doesn't feel like exercise." These Aerobic Prayers hold enormous appeal to a wide variety of people who do not think of themselves as dancers and who may not be interested in participating in formal exercise programs. These movements allow you to explore the body as prayer in the privacy of your home or personal space. They are safe and simplified versions of complex, traditional dances from all over the world.

The beauty of these movements is that you can make friends with your body in your own way and at your own pace. You can discover which gestures feel right and give you the sense of connection with your inner self that you're seeking. You can follow the movements and images in this book as I lay them out, but I hope that you will also be inspired to experiment with creating your own dances, motions, and prayers that express your own inner spirit, celebrate your blessings, and enhance your life.

In my and my students' experiences, these Aerobic Prayers can help you communicate with your own soul and discover your deepest feelings, longings, aspirations, and joy. Just as the practice of yoga or meditation enhances every moment of your day, I have found that the practice of prayerful dance extends into all my daily activities and infuses them with a heightened awareness. Everything I do becomes a moving meditation.

When you begin to put your spirit in action, you may at first have to overcome some inertia, which often shows up as a resistance to change and to trying something new. You may hear an inner voice saying, "I can't do this. I'm too tired. I'm too fat. I'm out of shape. I can't dance. I'll feel stupid." As I tell the participants in my workshops, there is no need to apologize for your initial inexperience. Don't worry about it. Trust. Trust your body to lead you to the right expression for you. Your movements will silence the inner critic. Focus on the pleasure of your body in motion. It's hard for worries and self-consciousness to bother you when you're moving around. Living in a body means, by definition, that you are working with limitations. Yet the Creator is working physically, emotionally, and spiritually through your limitations every moment of your life. This is, in fact, the glory of incarnation. We are perpetually offered the grace to grow and learn from our weaknesses and turn them into strengths.

If you feel a little awkward or uncomfortable when you first begin to practice *Spirit in Action*, feel free to stop, collect yourself, and start again. All movement begins in stillness. In fact, you may want to begin all your prayers with a moment of stillness. In this silent intent all possibilities of movement exist.

## ⌒ A Simple Mind-Body Exploration ⌒

*Stand up in the middle of a room so that you have enough space around you to move. Stand comfortably, feet shoulder-width apart, so that you are balanced with your weight equally distributed on both legs. Let your arms hang to the side. Breathe out and in slowly and deeply three times. Feel the stillness around you and within you. Be with the stillness for another few breaths. Allow the stillness, your breath, and body to direct your first movements. Perhaps you feel like slowly and meditatively walking around the room or simply walking in place, deliberately and gently lifting your foot, feeling the length of your foot as you slowly lift it inch by inch, heel to arch to ball to toes, and placing it down again, toe, ball, heel, as you repeat the motion with the other foot. Perhaps your arms want to move as if you were walking or your hands simply want to hold each other in front of you in a relaxed or prayerful gesture. Or perhaps as you continue to walk in place or slowly move around the room, your arms will want to raise themselves all the way up over your head and your eyes follow them.*

*Allow yourself to be guided from one step to the next, producing movements that come from your own inner awareness. They might be large, strong movements or small, gentle movements. These movements need not be "right" or look formal, as in ballet or jazz. Trust your body. When you move from your own soul, you radiate an energy that's beautiful in itself. Move in this meditation as long as you feel comfortable.*

# DANCING SPIRIT

I have had the opportunity to study and participate in many forms of dance in many different regions and countries around the world, including West Africa, the Congo, the Caribbean, Hawaii, Brazil, Haiti, and North Africa. I've studied hula, belly, and Sufi dancing, as well as Eastern sacred movement traditions such as tai chi, yoga, and qi gong. Whether studying at home in the San Francisco Bay area or seeing dances performed in their native settings, I have always been impressed by the many diverse ways that dance and movement serve both the individual and the community. Dance is a source of inspiration and rejuvenation; it can be a form of storytelling, history keeping, celebration, and social ritual. Quite often it is a mode of prayer.

This sacred aspect of dance, or moving for a "higher cause," particularly captivates me, and I have been fundamentally influenced by the many sacred dance forms I have studied. But my interpretation of the moving prayers in this book developed out of spontaneous expressions from my own spirit, in my own living room, coming through music that spoke to my heart. Ten years ago I began trying out different movements and discovered that I, too, could dance myself into a full and immediate spiritual experience, in which I was completely awake, alive, and conscious of the rush of energy or spirit moving within me. At that time I was meditating regularly and noticed that my personal meditative patterns changed. I attributed this to the new spiritual dances that were coming to me. After dancing, I could summon the calm, focused attention of meditation more easily and quickly. Because my body's energy was flowing clearly, my mind was more at ease. This improved ability to focus also helped my work as a chiropractor and enabled me to treat my patients more effectively. It increased my intuition as well and helped me diagnose the patients and find relief for the tensions they held in their bodies and minds.

This experience of attaining mind–body clarity and peace through movement was not entirely new to me. I had been a marathon runner in the early 1980s, and the altered state, or "runner's high," that comes from that aerobic activity was similar to the focus I felt after dancing. Back then I had noticed that my ability to meditate improved just after running, but I had not given it much thought and had not made running part of my spiritual regimen. One day a friend who is a minister happened to comment that he regularly meditated just after he ran, because he could do it more clearly and enter deeper states. Hearing this was like a bell of awakening. I realized in that moment that the body could become part of the centering experience of prayer and meditation. It actually assists in connecting to an Inner or Higher Source of energy or spirit. Instead of criticizing myself for fidgeting when I sat to meditate, I could systematically use physical activity to help me find a way through distractions and restlessness. Perhaps physical activity is the missing link that can help active Westerners maintain a regular meditation practice.

I hope that these methods of combining movement with prayer will give you, too, a powerful practice for expressing your own spirituality, for finding your own internal spiritual rhythm, and for moving with the pulse of the Universe.

Don't be surprised if, once unleashed, your own dancing spirit erupts spontaneously in its own dance of the joy of being. Come! Dance the Song of the Soul!

# Chapter 1

# MOVEMENT AS A SPIRITUAL PRACTICE

*Dance should be a divine expression of the human spirit.*
—ISADORA DUNCAN

Let us begin this exploration together with an embodied prayer, a form of sacred dance that helps us to express ourselves physically, by using our body together with our voice or inner thoughts—instead of spoken or silent prayer. The Heart of Attention, shown on the next page, is a gentle, thoughtful way to begin putting your spirit to work. Let the words in the captions guide you through the exercise.

Physical movement is the first of three basic components of moving spirit into action. The second is repetition. When you repeat moves *as* you repeat a prayer audibly or silently, the dance becomes a *moving meditation*. This repetition increases the energy of the movements and increases your emotional and muscle memory of the moves so that you can actually tap into the energy of those exercises later in the day. For example, the following prayer may be repeated six, eight, or ten times, depending on your level of comfort. You can practice it slowly as if it were a tai chi meditation, or you might try doing it to a fast, rhythmic piece of music. Rhythm is the third basic component of putting spirit into action. When you move to a fast beat, accelerating movement and therefore heart rate, the moving meditation becomes an Aerobic Prayer. Mind! Body! Action!

*We bring
the fullness of
our attention . . .*

*. . . to a single
point of
attention . . .*

## ∼ The Heart of Attention ∼

*To do this embodied prayer, begin standing with feet hip-width apart, arms at your sides, and begin to become aware of your surroundings. Inhale and exhale three times and feel yourself firmly connected to the ground. Slowly lift your hands up above your head, palms up. Then gently bring your hands together over your head, and hold for ten seconds. Take a few even breaths, then slowly lower your hands from above your head to the heart level. Let your eyes follow the motion of your hands. Feel the stillness for three counts, and when you're ready, press your hands forward, palms out, making a commitment to act from your heart in all you do today. Take a moment to breathe deeply in and out, feeling the strength of a mind-body prayer. When you've practiced this sequence a couple of times, you can add a slow, marching step in place to promote a feeling of connection to the earth.*

The way you decide to express an embodied prayer makes it your personal sacred dance. Taking movements that you like to do and combining them to create prayer is what I will teach you throughout this book.

*. . . within
the
heart.*

*May all the actions that my hands touch
this day come from this point of attention,
a reflection of spirit in action.*

All of life is animated by spiritual rhythms. We see and feel them in the steady beating of the heart, in the cycles of nature, in the dance of waves in water, in the patterns of particle physics, and in the steady in and out of the breath. Through our own bodies' rhythms and movement, we participate in universal rhythms.

Yet just as no two people can have exactly the same life experiences, no two individuals can dance the same steps with the same style, emotional qualities, or depth of soul. Even professional dancers interpret the same role differently, so that performances change from cast to cast. The path of sacred dance and the path of life experience allow many different nuances, many dips and detours. The spiritual process, the awakening of mind and body, is a journey. In order to begin dancing the path, you have to take a first step.

This means that you can practice *Spirit in Action* at your own pace, in accordance with who you are and where you are now in your life. Embodied prayer can help you focus more on the things that matter to you by raising your level of concentration. It helps you live more fully in the present moment, increase your clarity of purpose, and learn to discern meaning in encounters and circumstances. Our lives move at such a fast clip that it becomes ever more difficult to feel peaceful and centered. Moving meditations can help you slow down and make more of your time. Think about the map you use at the local mall to find the store you're looking for. Next to a bright red circle that marks your location are the words *You are here*. Think about holding on to those three simple words wherever you are in your daily life. You are nowhere else but here. Focus. Attention. Concentration. Let embodied prayer be an aid in getting you *here*.

At times prayer and meditation come as naturally as breath, and at other times the noisy mind won't cease its incessant chatter. Conscious movement can help you enter more easily into a prayerful state that promotes self-understanding and spiritual growth. We fall and rise up. We contract and expand, withdraw and reach forward. We alternate between attempts at control and resistance and the surrender of "Thy will be done." We clutch and release, move with focused intention, and we can dance in wild abandon.

Through embodied prayer, we become more aware of our movements and what they reveal about our innermost feelings. We are constantly sending messages out into the world and need to be aware of how we move and why. By moving consciously, we bring spiritual focus into our world. Just as we can allow certain movements to reflect our inner experiences, so we can also choose movements that direct our mental focus toward spirituality. To illustrate this, consider a basic motion of our everyday lives we often take for granted: walking. Vietnamese monk and author Thich Nhat Hanh teaches a walking meditation, a lovely, simple example of embodied spiritual focus.

### ∼ Walking Meditation ∼

*To do a walking meditation, breathe in and out slowly and evenly three times. Pick a point to which you will walk, and form the intention that as you walk, you are blessing with your feet the earth, your mother, on whom you are walking. Pick up your foot slowly and step forward, feeling every inch of your foot gently stepping onto Mother Earth—heel, instep, ball, toes. As your one foot comes into full presence on the ground, slowly step again with the other foot, blessing the earth, the floor—giving thanks for the nurturing she has given you. When you have reached your destination, turn around and return to where you began. As you walk, keep your mind focused on your feet and your breathing. Imagine that you are leaving footprints behind, as if you were walking on a sandy beach.*

*Thich Nhat Hanh says that we can leave footprints of worry and stress on the earth as we walk, or we can choose to leave the imprints of peace. What do you choose to leave on the earth today? As Nhat Hanh writes in* Peace Is Every Step*: "Are you massaging our Mother Earth every time your foot touches her? Are you planting seeds of joy and peace? I try to do exactly that with every step, and I know that our Mother Earth is most appreciative. Peace is every step. Shall we continue our journey?"*

By moving consciously, we become a vehicle for spirit in action. Spirit is made flesh through our actions and movements in everyday life.

# THE SACRED CIRCLE OF SPIRITUAL QUALITIES

Everything the Power of the World
does is done in a circle. The sky is
round and I have heard that the earth is
round like a ball and so are all the stars.
The wind, in its greatest power, whirls.
Birds make their nests in circles,
for theirs is the same religion as ours.
The sun comes forth and goes down again
in a circle. The moon does the
same and both are round. Even the
seasons form a great circle in their
changing and always come back again
to where they were. The life of a man
is a circle from childhood to childhood.
And so it is in everything where power moves.
—BLACK ELK, OGLALA SIOUX (1863–1950)
FROM *THE LOOP*, BY NICHOLAS EVANS

Many sacred dances around the world are performed in a circle. In many Native American traditions, the circle is a symbol for life passing through the generations, for the one Source of Divinity within all beings, and for the equality that exists between all members of the circle. The sacred circle symbolizes that much of life is lived in a cyclical pattern, spiritually and biologically. Our bodies have their own daily, monthly, and yearly rhythms, and we observe these rhythms within the context of social, cultural, and religious calendars that are themselves related to the seasonal cycle of winter to spring to summer to fall. Annually the cycle repeats, but we've advanced another year in age, and hopefully in wisdom and maturity.

The prayerful dances I have developed are meant to evoke and teach four primary spiritual qualities: intention, gratitude, forgiveness, and acceptance. I envision these qualities on a circle that has been divided into four quadrants, each containing one of the spiritual qualities. As we learn to embody these qualities, we gain in self-understanding, we become more whole spiritually, and we learn to give expression to the unique rhythms of our individual experience. And just as these attributes help us to put spirit in action, there are active, physical prayers that help us embody these virtues.

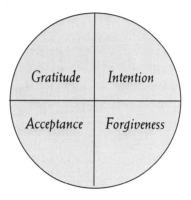

As we travel around the circle of spiritual development, we enter into ever-deepening levels of consciousness. Each *revolution* brings you closer to your own personal spiritual *evolution*. The top half of the circle is divided into gratitude and intention. On the bottom are forgiveness and acceptance. We begin and end with gratitude.

## GRATITUDE

Gratitude is the most centered, joyful, and pleasant quality to develop. I personally feel that it is the most important spiritual quality to develop. It is certainly the path of a happy heart. Gratitude gives us a sense of fullness in our lives that makes us want to grow and reach out to others. From the fullness of gratitude we become inspired and motivated to affirm new goals and take appropriate action to fulfill a healing, higher vision of the world.

Author, lecturer, and pastor, the Reverend George McLaird once said that the only truly valid prayer is one of gratitude. Gratitude is not always easy to practice, but we can start by practicing moment-by-moment thankfulness. If we can come to believe that every person we encounter, every trouble and blessing we undergo, is for our soul's highest purpose, then we can come to see all experience as a blessing. In the face of any loss, we can be grateful for our own life, our family, the trees, the air, the quiet snows, the return of spring, the warmth of the sun, even the richness of our emotions and tears.

Everything and anything in our lives can bring our attention to the present moment. Just as the Eskimos have more than a dozen words for snow, gratitude comes in many different shapes and sizes. Mother Teresa used a mantra as she went about her daily duties: "And this, too." In a television documentary, she explained that this was a contraction of "And God is in this, too. I am grateful for this experience." She ministered everywhere to people whom no one else would even touch. She saw the light of their souls and was grateful for being able to experience God in every person she met.

We, too, can be grateful for all the gifts of creation and experience that we are given. Through gratitude we affirm, "Yes, I am alive to my life!"

Try the following simple, elegant gesture for embodying a prayer of gratitude.

## ∿ Gratitude Gesture ∿

*First, name something for which you are grateful today. As you name it, touch your heart with both hands, then open your arms and hands out to the sides. This simple gesture physically opens your body in an attitude of reception and vulnerability. It allows you to embrace the fullness of your life with humility and thankfulness. By using our bodies physically to express gratitude, we become more fully alive to the wonder of the present moment. We become cocreators of our spirituality with the God force. Repeat this naming and prayerful movement ten times or more.*

We tend to attract more of those things in our lives for which we are already grateful. For example, when you are appreciative of the relationships in your life, you tend to put more time and care into their nurturance and development. It's no big mystery that relationships flourish under these conditions. If you are grateful for your health, you will more likely affirm your gratitude by maintaining the habits and lifestyle that support it. Some people take this idea even further by saying that we actually become magnetic to that which we think about and for which we are grateful.

In *Conversations with God*, Neale Donald Walsch illustrates this idea:

> You will not have that for which you ask, nor can you have anything you want. This is because your very request is a statement of lack, and your saying that you want a thing only works to produce that precise experience "wanting" in your reality. The correct prayer is, therefore, never a prayer of supplication, but a prayer of gratitude. . . . Thankfulness is thus the most powerful statement to God; an affirmation that even before you have asked, I have answered. Therefore never supplicate. *Appreciate.*

Our need to express gratitude for our lives, to reach out from ourselves to a Higher Power and to others is innate. Spirit by nature is expansive. This impetus for expansion leads us to the quality of intention, the next quadrant in the circle of spiritual virtues.

## INTENTION

> The thought manifests as the word;
> The word manifests as the deed;
> The deed develops into habit;
> And habit hardens into character.
> So watch the thought and its ways with care.
> And let it spring from love
> Born out of concern for all beings.
> —THE BUDDHA, FROM *LIFE PRAYERS*, EDITED
> BY ELIZABETH ROBERTS AND ELIAS AMIDON

Intention is the process of focusing your mental energy. You focus on that which you are creating and invest all your thoughts and actions with the intention of fulfilling your goal. You simultaneously see yourself as having fulfilled the goal *and* as successfully completing each step along the way to its fulfillment. Intention is the mental energy that eliminates distractions and keeps you grounded in your endeavors. It is closely related to visualization and affirmation and can use both these practices. You visualize by holding in your mind's eye an image of what you desire, and you see it as already existing. You also affirm that you are fulfilling your intention.

Affirmations can help you accomplish spiritual intentions as well as material ones. This one from *Meditations to Heal Your Life*, by Louise Hay, is one of my favorites: "Peace begins with me. If I want to live in a peaceful world, then it is up to me to make sure I am a peaceful person. No matter how others behave, I keep peace in my heart. I declare peace in the midst of chaos or madness. I surround all difficult situations with peace and love." When you set clear intentions and affirm them with positive language, your daily actions will come into alignment with your powerful mental images. This brings into physical reality that which you have already created in your heart and mind. The embodiment of the prayers and affirmations that we'll be exploring throughout this book will help you clarify and empower your own spiritual intentions, and your intentions will help your practice of putting spirit in action. The circle of spiritual qualities is a positive feedback system!

In the contemporary West, the creative power of visualization, affirmation, and intention is seen in the acceptance of ideas such as Norman Vincent Peale's "Power of Positive Thinking" and Christian intercessory prayer, which hold that change can take place by maintaining a positive picture of the intended outcome. The Unity Church expresses the same thought this way: "That which we think about is sure to come about." This may seem overly simplistic at first, but several scientific studies have shown a link between mental intention and physical effect.

Intention is the key to changing your thinking to become more purposeful in your living. Intention engages your will to choose thoughts and actions that reflect your highest aspirations, hopes, dreams, and prayers. Taking intention one step further, you can physically embody them in gestures and movements as you mentally affirm or visualize them.

Here is an example of how this can work. The following exercise embodies the physical and spiritual qualities associated with the act of reaching. A reaching motion in a dance prayer can be associated with reaching toward the distant horizons of our highest dreams or with sending the light of spiritual wisdom to the far corners of the world. We then might translate the simple act of reaching for a cup in the cupboard or for shampoo in the shower as an act that is part of our greater purpose. For some people reaching will translate to confidence and belief in the future of their highest dream. For others it is the notion of sending light to the healing of all beings that will translate as a reminder that they are on a path of service. Each dancer's experience of every movement will be unique to his or her own inner evolution and place on the journey. The dances help us to cultivate and translate inner strength and consciousness into spiritual action and mindfulness in everyday acts of living.

## ⌒ Reaching Exercise ⌒

*You can perform this reaching exercise either standing or sitting. First, name an intention, a goal, or your highest aspiration. Reach your dominant hand out to the far horizon palm down. Imagine that you are sending the energy of creation out from your fingertips, turning the possibility of your aspiration into reality. Let your eyes follow the stream of energy you are sending. Continue to send your mental energy, your breath, and your positive intention. See the picture of this dream as fulfilled. Now turn your hand over palm up and envision yourself holding the completed image of that which you intend to create in the palm of your hand. What does it look like? Is there anything within the image you would like to change? Do so now. Pull the finished image into your heart center, planting it there as a seed by pressing your palm over your heart. Allow your breath to feed the seedling. Continue to think of this seedling growing in the fertile soil of your heart and form the further intention that you offer the prayer of your breathing into it*

*again and again until it is accomplished in fact. Stay in this visualization for as long as you like. You may find that you want to breathe into this image from time to time during your day. You can send thought energy to this intention whenever you please.*

The preceding process is called by several names in various traditions. Some Buddhist, Hindu, and Hawaiian Huna practitioners refer to it as feeding *prana*, or life force, to your prayer. All of these traditions share the belief that there is life force, referred to variously as chi or prana, inherent in the breath. By using body-mind imagery supported by the breath, you can supply more energy to visualized intentions. Here is a simple exercise in kinesiology that demonstrates the power of intention.

## ∼ Energy and Strength ∼

*Work with a partner. Hold your arm out from your shoulder at about 90 degrees to your side. Now have your partner try to push it down while you resist as strongly as you can. Notice how much force he or she has to use to push your arm down. Then both of you relax. Drop your arm to the side. Shake it out. Then extend your arm out to the side again as before, only this time visualize that you are shooting a stream of energy out from your fingertips into the distance, right through the wall of the room to the far horizon. Focus on the stream of powerful energy you are sending out through your arm. Now have your partner try to push your arm down again and notice that he or she has much more difficulty doing it, if indeed your partner can do it at all. By visualizing the stream of energy shooting out through your arm, you have embodied your intention to keep it in place, extended from your side.*

You can actively choose and strengthen your intentions, or you can allow your focus to be distracted by the many concerns of daily life. You can choose to infuse everything you do with the peacefulness of honorable intention. Here's an example. You can walk in a shopping mall and be attracted by many of the items that are beckoning to you from the attractively displayed merchandise. Or you can take the same walk in the mall while holding the intention "I have enough. I am content." Try it in the supermarket when any number of unhealthy products are trying to leap into your cart. When you actively choose your focus, you are living in a state of spiritual empowerment. You are alive to the fact that you have the power to choose your internal focus rather than being buffeted by the prevailing winds of external circumstances and stimuli.

In her book *Minding the Body, Mending the Mind*, Dr. Joan Borysenko cites several studies that illustrate the powerful effect of the mind on healing. In one study of the effects of a new chemotherapy drug on women, one third of the women who received only a placebo (sugar pill) still lost their hair! In another study fifty-seven women were followed for ten years after undergoing mastectomies for breast cancer. Of the women who demonstrated a feisty attitude, who actively sought to help themselves heal, 55 percent were alive and well after ten years. Of those who were passive or fatalistic, only 22 percent were alive in ten years.

A controversial study in the 1950s underscores the powerful role the mind has in healing. Dr. Bruno Klopfer was treating a patient who was clearly in the final advanced stages of cancer and was literally on his deathbed, barely able to even breathe without an oxygen mask. The drug Krebiozen was just being released as a possible cancer treatment, and Dr. Klopfer administered it to his patient, who accepted the treatment with much enthusiasm and hope. Within ten days the patient's tumors had "melted like snowballs," and he was released from the hospital. Shortly thereafter Krebiozen was discredited by physicians and regarded as perfectly useless. Within two months the patient relapsed to his original condition. Dr. Klopfer, suspecting that the patient's belief was affecting his illness, fabricated a "new, improved" form of Krebiozen and with much fanfare began a series of injections that consisted only of water. The patient made a second astonishing recovery, even more quickly than his first. Symptom free for more than two months, the patient was leading a normal life when the AMA released a news report to the public that Krebiozen had been a dismal failure in the treatment of cancer. Within a few days, the patient relapsed and died.

Author Larry Dossey, M.D., has written frequently on the effects of intercessory prayer, which is praying for the health and well-being of another person, particularly if he or she is ill or having surgery. It has been demonstrated over and over again that people are more likely to get well if other people offer prayers for their recovery. Even bacteria growing in petri dishes have flourished and multiplied at a faster rate when prayer is directed to their well-being, compared to organisms for which no one prayed. This is not a supernatural phenomenon but most likely an interaction between the energy fields of different organisms that we don't yet understand.

Even with the best of intentions, of course, random events still happen. Though we fully intend to drive safely to work when we get up in the morning, most of us have not yet evolved to the point at which we can feel comfortable canceling our auto insurance. We can attempt to guide the large and small actions of our lives toward a favorable outcome by reinforcing them with positive intention.

If we are reasonably sure that our attitudes, thoughts, and intentions affect how our lives and dreams unfold, then we should also examine the images and beliefs that we allow into our heads. A friend of mine says he only allows himself one hour of news per day. He calls it "one great hour of depression," and he rations the steady barrage of negative events that the media feels compelled to present. Choose to limit your exposure to this kind of material. Listen to good music instead of your TV. Talk with your family. Read more. Dance more. Notice how powerful it feels to pay attention only to ideas that nourish and reflect your intentions.

## FORGIVENESS

Our personal internal process of self-discovery and spiritual cultivation is ultimately meant to lead us to be able to connect to each other, to the earth, and to Divine Energy. Forgiveness is key to this personal and spiritual growth as well as to inner peace. When we are bogged down in past resentments, we are unable to feel peaceful or act peacefully. To have peace in this moment and to bring peace to others, we must let go of past anger, betrayals, and indignation, no matter how righteous our feelings may be.

But forgiveness can be oh so difficult! It is even more difficult if we have been carrying ill feelings for years. Anger and resentment can straitjacket our hearts and affect all areas of our lives and relationships. Of all the processes we will move through in this book, forgiveness can be the hardest.

Most of the time when an issue arises between people, groups, or nations, it does so because one group or person believes that his or her way of being, thinking, or acting is right and the other's way of being, thinking, or acting is wrong.

Forgiveness begins with the willingness to ask ourselves, "Do I want to be right, or do I want to create peace? Do I want to be right, or do I want to be happy?" The small-*t* personal truth of the moment may be that we petulantly want to be right. However, to have the capital-*T* higher Truth, peace needs to be acknowledged as our highest goal.

To forgive others effectively, we also need to forgive ourselves for our shortcomings. Being regretful or feeling guilty for words we spoke thoughtlessly or things we did or neglected to do many years ago—or even days ago—is emotionally and spiritually unhealthy. The weight of self-recrimination can feel as if a forty-pound sack were pressing down on our head or shoulders, impeding us from moving forward, making us slump in dejection and remorse. When the soul is weighted down like that, the body reflects those feelings in thought and posture. As author and motivational teacher Caroline Myss says, "Your biography becomes your biology." You need to forgive yourself and others in order to possess your own soul and energy fully.

Neil Douglas-Klotz teaches a new view of forgiveness for ourselves and others in *Prayers of the Cosmos*, in which he translates the Lord's Prayer from the original Aramaic language, which Jesus is believed to have spoken. The line "Forgive us our debts (trespasses) as we forgive our debtors (those who trespass against us)" is interpreted as "Loose the cords of mistakes binding us, as we release the strands we hold of others' guilt." I love this version and the sense it gives that letting go of what ties us up in knots is the essence of forgiveness, blessing, and connecting to the One Source.

When we are not willing to forgive ourselves or others, our minds and lives become limited, as if trapped behind a glass that is completely fogged. When we do not forgive ourselves, the fog is on the inside of the glass. When we can't forgive another, the fog is on the outside. The net result is the same. We see ourselves as separate. We are prevented from seeing the truth of our oneness—that we are manifestations of the same Spirit. Although we will always make mistakes as we progress through life, the only way to learn from them is through forgiveness.

Forgiveness and self-forgiveness are indications that we believe that we are connected to each other and to the One. When we do not practice forgiveness, we act against unity and harmony. Forgiveness is granted as a fact of life. In *The Path* author William Cozzolino says, "But Jesus never did forgive sins. He knew that judgment was an internal process. He simply stated the fact: 'Your sins are forgiven.' "

Forgiveness does not mean that you allow yourself to be abused by words or actions. You have to maintain a healthy boundary between yourself and others and refuse to tolerate behavior that threatens your physical or emotional safety. You can forgive someone for past behavior but should make sure that you will not be exposed to further unacceptable behavior from that person. The process of forgiveness is meant to heal the inner fragmentation of the soul that often outlasts injury, trauma, or abuse.

Dance can help get our bodies, minds, and spirits aligned so that we can practice true forgiveness and experience the simple joy of a peaceful heart. A dance I choreographed and set to a poem and song entitled "Prayer for the Warriors" (see the "Musical Resources" section in the back of the book) calls for peace within and peace in the world. The song's refrain is, "May the warriors find peace within. May the healing of the world begin." Let's try to embody peace with this dance now.

## ∽ Prayer for the Warriors ∽

*Begin with your feet about shoulder-width apart. Make two fists, raise them to the level of your head or higher, and bang them twice into the air as if you were banging on a door. Then lower your fists and bang them twice as if you were banging on a table. Allow yourself to feel the energy of contracted anger that comes with this movement. Notice how your chest and breathing feel. Then extend your arms and hands to each side with a fluid motion, which opens the chest and heart area. Notice how this motion changes and releases your breath as well as the contraction of the chest and heart area.*

*Bring your hands back to the area of the heart and imagine that you are now holding the beloved planet Earth between your hands. Send the energy of your personal prayer for healing and peace out to all beings and to the earth itself. Visualize healing: "May the healing of the earth begin." Visualize peace.*

*I like to repeat this embodied prayer ten to thirty times. Whenever you decide you are complete with it, hold for a few moments in stillness in the prayer for the earth and the community of all beings. Blessed be.*

Prayer for the Warriors is a simple, beautiful series of gestures to use to evoke inner peace. It is a powerful physical prayer for moving blocked energy or anger out of your life, and it helps move your spirit into forgiveness. When you remember or review old resentments and anger, your breathing usually gets shallow, your heart speeds up, your vision narrows. This dance breaks up that blocked-up, deadened feeling with jagged initial movements and pushes them out away from you, allowing room for new healing energy to enter your heart.

The next time you feel angered by an old slight or a new problem, remember that you can choose *not* to express anger. You can breathe and affirm that your inner being is timeless, eternal, and always at peace. You can choose to tap into this inner reservoir of peace. You can sing or chant or count to ten. Or you can move, physically traveling away from the trigger of your anger, and resolve the tension by stretching your body and mind out of clenched posture. Moving is usually the most direct and powerful path out of the spin cycle of anger, and dancing the Prayer for the Warriors can be an effective prayer for healing and peace when you are angry or agitated. Although you may first identify more with the angry energy of your fists, and resist opening yourself into the fluid, openhearted movement of traveling back to your heart center, just make yourself do it. Even if it feels weird and difficult to open into this softer pattern when you are angry, trust the wisdom of your body to help you. Your body remembers how much better it feels to let go into relaxation and peace. Just keep putting the energy in motion while holding the line "May the warriors [in this case you] find peace within." Slowly but surely the energy of the anger will begin to peel off like onion skin. This moving meditation for healing and peace will bring you home to yourself quicker than you might expect. The movement combines the physical language of moving from hardness to flowing softness, with open breathing and clear mental intention. All systems are integrated, drawing you back to the healing of forgiveness and the Great Mystery of your Spirit center.

## ACCEPTANCE

Acceptance of our lives, of ourselves, and of others is the fourth primary spiritual quality. Gaining the attitude of acceptance requires that we become comfortable with the fact that we are part of a Great Mystery. We acknowledge that a higher order of wisdom is at work in our lives. Although we consciously try to create the circumstances and direction of our lives, we are clearly not in total control. Much as we think we know what is best, our souls will often be redirected into unexpected pathways for our unfolding.

On the surface, acceptance and conscious intention may seem mutually exclusive. How can we hold an intention to change our lives and the world around us while at the same time accepting the world as is? This is the paradox of acceptance. In order to become accepting, we have to cultivate a level of trust that what we have been given is exactly what we need for the greatest good in the development of our soul. We can ask of every situation and experience, "What is there for me to learn in this?" When we truly trust the process of life even when it doesn't match our preconceptions for how it should unfold, we are grounded and able to balance and make peace between opposites.

The more attached we are to the life course we attempt to select for ourselves, the more difficult it will be to learn acceptance. To cultivate acceptance, we have to look beyond the limitations of our human condition—to see the unity that connects us to each other and to our Source.

Sometimes it is only with the wisdom of time that you can look back and appreciate how exquisitely your life has unfolded. Perhaps you have been disappointed by not getting a job you really wanted, only to find a much better one down the road. If you had gotten the first job, you would not have been in the right place at the right time for the better plan to work itself out. Perhaps you had your heart broken by a lover, but with the benefit of time, you have come to recognize that it would have been a terrible, even more painful match. In my college and graduate school days, I was always anxious and struggling financially. I learned firsthand what it is to be panicky about meeting bare survival needs. Although these were lessons I detested at the time, the experience gave me a deep empathy and compassion for my financially challenged patients over the years. Clearly my own experience softened my heart for the struggling parent who comes to my office today with an injured child.

Some of our finest lessons are purchased through our difficulties. An unhealed relationship can be a particular challenge as we try to navigate the course between forgiveness and acceptance. By working at acceptance, we can come to an appreciation for the lessons the relationship has taught us and be grateful for them, once again returning home to gratitude on the circle of spiritual qualities. Through acceptance we move beyond forgiveness, beyond the willingness to release, and actually plumb the experience for life lessons. The recognition of powerful life lessons grants us release and allows us to move on with our life.

The challenge in practicing acceptance is to learn to trust that there are no mistakes in our life, that we can learn from everything that occurs to us and find meaning in all our experiences. To trust, give up the beliefs and illusions you hold. You are exactly where you need to be in this moment, in this place. If you are in pain, the question is not only "How do I get away from this pain?" but also "What can this pain and situation teach me?" From the point at which we can see a larger meaning or the potential for a larger meaning, we can practice acceptance and become free to move on. From this perspective, we are also able to return to gratitude.

"Thank you for this learning. Thank you for this deepening of my soul." We are able to make meaning out of most, if not all, of our experiences. Within this gratitude lies our evolving sense of peace.

# EMBODIED PRAYERS FOR GRATITUDE, INTENTION, FORGIVENESS, AND ACCEPTANCE

I like to use the following series of movements to invoke the sacred circle of spiritual qualities. There are four separate body prayers that make up this sequence. I prefer to do them in the order in which they are given. However, you may find that there are some days when you will want to work on only one quality. Feel free to practice them according to your inner promptings or in response to the promptings of challenges in your daily life.

## ～ Gratitude ～

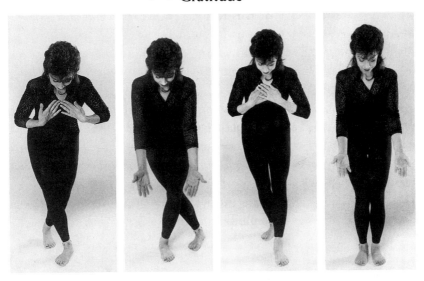

*Gratitude is the alpha and omega point of the circle. We begin and end with gratitude. In this dance, I like to name my blessings and remember the joys in my life.*

*Begin standing in a neutral position, with your feet together. Cross your right foot in front of your left and bring your fingertips to your heart. Name a blessing in your life. Then cross your left foot in front of your right and move your hands away from your heart in a gesture of thanksgiving, palms facing front, fingers pointing toward the earth. Name another. Bring your fingertips back to your heart and step back with your right foot into your starting position. Your left foot also returns to the starting position, as you repeat the hand gesture with palms facing front, fingers to the earth.*

*Next, repeat the same step leading with your left foot. Your fingers again touch your heart as your left foot crosses in front of your right. Your fingers open toward the earth in the same gesture of gratitude as your right foot crosses in front of your left. Touch your heart once more and return your left foot to the starting position and open your palms to the earth once more as your right foot returns to its starting position.*

*Repeat the sequence, alternating sides, as many times as you like as you name your blessings. I like to get into a rhythm that is upbeat and happy for this dance. African drumming rhythms are a favorite of mine. I will typically repeat the sequence fifty to sixty times, but as you learn the dance, do what is comfortable for you. About ten to fifteen times might be more enjoyable, although it might take you four or five repetitions to get the steps going automatically. This is a joyful step. Let your body give thanks for your blessings.*

## ∼ Intention ∼

*The following steps will help you develop the power of focus. The first part of the gesture creates the picture of your goal or desired creation. The second part uses a pointing movement borrowed from a Brazilian dance to direct energy into the fulfillment of the intention. In this tradition, pointing is a powerful act of will. As you point, imagine that you are sending energy from your fingertips to infuse the object with which you are connecting—in this case your intentions. In a sense, you are willing it to come to you.*

*Stand up and begin by stepping in place with small, unhurried steps. Feel yourself connecting to the earth, to your own inner rhythm, or think of a rhythm from a piece of music you like. Bring your hands in front of your body, a little above your waist. Imagine you are holding a six- to ten-inch*

*bubble between the palms of your hands. Place the image or picture of your intention inside this bubble. Be as clear and definite about the details of your visualization as possible. Allow your hands to play back and forth around the bubble as you continue to visualize your intention. Visualize the release of this image and let it hover in the air as you create the next movement. Point with your dominant hand, arm extended in front of you at shoulder level. Begin to turn 360 degrees as you point and make an abrupt stop while pointing to the imaginary bubble that holds your intention. Send the image energy through the tip of your pointing finger. Then reach with your left hand and pull the image into your heart center and hold it there with both hands. You can repeat this exercise, but often one time with heightened focus will feel like enough. Throughout the day bring your breath into this image that has been "seeded" in your heart.*

## ∽ Forgiveness ∽

*The next steps are helpful when you are faced with an issue or a person whom you want to forgive. This step is meant to release the cords of resentment and guilt that bind us and invokes the energy of forgiveness. As you repeat the following step, try to envision yourself feeling free as you release the cords of resentment. The gesture is symbolic of untying a knot that is holding you in bondage. Let it go and allow your mind and body to feel the freedom that comes from release.*

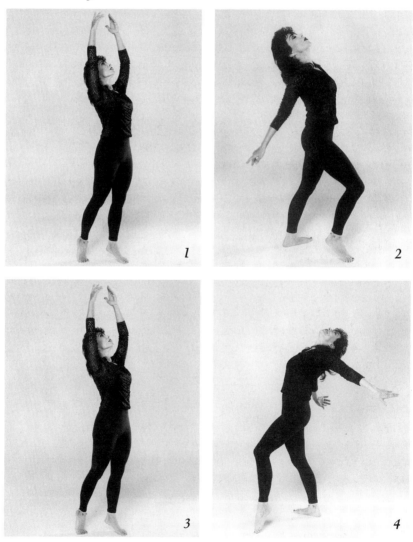

*Begin with your hands reaching above your head, facing front with your feet about shoulder-width apart. Step behind with your left foot. Your body will naturally turn slightly left. As you step behind, bring your hands down and extend them and your arms all the way down and back, behind your hips, fingertips pointing to the earth. As your hands pass over your body, imagine that they are cleansing any feelings of anger, guilt, and resentment, releasing them into the earth. Repeat this simple step on alternating sides. Feel the energy of release and freedom this engenders.*

*There is no set number of times to do this dance. I sometimes repeat the steps fifty to a hundred times until I feel I have really come to terms with an issue or a person I want to forgive. Try this step about ten to twenty times at first and know that you can return to it and do it until you feel you have achieved a sense of completion.*

## ∿ Acceptance ∿

*The next steps evoke the energy of acceptance and help make peace with the mystery of life. Allow yourself to stop trying to understand why everything happens as it does. Trust in the goodness and greater purpose of the Universe and feel the comfort that can come to you when you open yourself to being part of a larger mystery.*

*Begin standing with your feet together. Step to the right and reach right at shoulder level. Leave your right hand extended as your right foot returns to its starting position. Then step left and reach left with your left hand at your shoulder level, leaving your left hand there as your left foot returns to neutral. These movements symbolize the confusion that arises when you are*

*pulled in two different directions. Then step front with your right foot and bring your hands to the sides of your head to symbolize the gaining of wisdom from what we are given. Bring your right foot back to the starting position. As your feet come back to the starting position, bring your hands down in front, palms facing front, fingers pointing to the earth as a gesture of humility and acceptance.*

*The series ends as it began with a return to the dance of gratitude for all the richness of our life experiences, the highs and the lows, for the wisdom they bring us. You can omit the footwork and simply touch your hands to your heart and open your hands to acknowledge your joys.*

I believe this series of simple dances represents the pattern for a whole life well lived. These four qualities, common to many spiritual traditions, are also the basis on which I have developed many of the dances that I teach. When I am in doubt in my life, I have found that these four simple dances have always helped me to find my way back to a place of peace, balance, and compassion.

# Chapter 2

# SACRED DANCE AROUND THE WORLD

How soon after humans learned to walk did they also begin to dance? I believe that they developed both activities almost simultaneously and that dance actually helped our ancestors learn about the innate power of their bodies. Through dance, they became more conscious of being in their bodies, of being physical beings. Even before developing language, according to anthropologists, our ancestors communicated with their bodies, using them to convey information and emotion, send out warnings in the form of attitude and posture, and show love and acceptance. Speech, believed to be a later arrival on the evolutionary scene, was integrated into existing physical forms of communication. Dance, story, and song became the way each generation preserved its culture for the next before the first written signs or pictographs were struck on rock and imprinted on clay.

The medium of the body, even today, is often the message. The body is a veritable dictionary of movement, encompassing a range of emotions and gestures from A to Z. As we'll discuss later on, the body is in perfect sync with what's going on inside us. Self-assurance is reflected in a confident walk, whereas upsetting emotions cling to the body like barnacles to a ship, sinking us into uncomfortable attitudes and postures. "Movement never lies," Martha Graham's father told her when she was a child, because he could tell by her posture when she wasn't being forthcoming or truthful. The vocabulary of movement can be as varied and unique as the cultures from which it arises or the bodies that enunciate it. The internal purpose that gives rise to gestures can

*Traditional Hawaiian Dance*

be shared among dancers or given a distinctive nuance and style by an individual's movements.

You do not have to be an accomplished dancer or a dance historian to be able to appreciate how movement speaks to us and through us. The movements that are offered for your exploration in this book have been borrowed from many different cultures. Some of the steps and gestures are repeated in their tra-

ditional form, and some are adapted to expressions that I found true for me. I developed certain gestures after having seen a performance or even a photo of a dance form with which I had been unfamiliar. With a sense of play and wonder, I have mimicked the posture or movement to discover what the movement represented to me or what internal emotional state it evoked. For example, there is a Hawaiian gesture used in traditional hula in which one hand is placed by the mouth and the other hand extends far away from the mouth. Traditionally this is a gesture that indicates speaking or calling out. For me it is a lovely stretching gesture to call to Spirit and begin a dance or meditative sequence. In my own personal use, the gesture became an invocation. You, too, can develop your own personal language of movement in prayer.

Throughout history people have used physical movements to help them intensify their expression of feelings of gratitude and celebration in private and public worship. The Old Testament's King David, in divine communion with the Creator, when the ark of the covenant was brought before him, danced his worship, according to 2 Samuel 6:14. Movement gives the prayer a physical intention, sending it out into the world. The energy of prayer goes through the body like electricity through copper wires, stimulating every cell and synapse, from head to toe. Physical movement intensifies this energy flow within us and around us.

Movement can be added to prayer to bestow blessings on others, to pray for guidance from a Higher Power, and to help form a connection to Divine

Power. These movements—which can be as quiet and simple as clasping hands and kneeling, or as rigorous and intricate as advanced yoga postures, or as dynamic as a whirling dervish or an ecstatic Shaker—all help us feel the Holy Spirit. In contrast, prayerful movements can be intense and stately, as in the formal routines of qi gong or tai chi, or they can be spontaneous movements that ask for guidance and blessing or offer thanks and gratitude. I call each of these practices "sacred dance"—the use of movement and prayer together to express reverence, celebration, and divine connection. Mindful movement serves many purposes and is endemic to many cultures, but I like to think that it is as relevant to today's fast-changing technological society as it was to our ancestors' more stable, parochial lives. As you can see from all these practices, spirit can be put in action whenever you want, wherever you are.

Meditation and prayer have been combined with kneeling, standing, sitting, and walking, in rhythmic sequences that sometimes use music as accompaniment. In African, Polynesian, Middle Eastern, Native American, Asian, Celtic, and Teutonic cultures, people realized that movement during prayer helped bring them closer to each other and closer to that which they considered divine. In the "grand entry" of the intertribal Native American powwow, for instance, the dancers move in a clockwise manner as each tribe, or family within the tribe, dances together. The elders lead the way, followed by children, grandchildren, and great-grandchildren, to symbolize the inheritance of the dancing spiritual tradition through the generations. Victor LaSarte, tribal elder from the Coeur d'Alene tribe, said at the 1999 powwow, "We're here to honor each other, respect each other, and show what the Creator put us here for, and to live in harmony." Sacred dance helps us connect to ourselves, to one another, and to the Divine. Ask yourself now, How high can I reach?

*Cherokee Medicine Woman Mary Sunbeam*
*Offering a Native American Blessing*

In some traditions—such as Balinese, Cambodian, and Indian—the dances enable the dancer to enter a mystical state of consciousness. The dance and the state of awareness that it catalyzes and communicates have the power to change the individual dancer and her onlookers. All will carry with them from the dance a heightened awareness into their everyday lives.

In sacred dance, movements become a physical prayer and the body a holy instrument. You embody the Divine. Dance moves you out of your head, out of your mental preoccupations, and into a direct experience of your body. It energizes the mind-body connection and fuses the body-mind with spirit. Sacred dance—or almost any dance—is spirit in action: lush, reverent, exuberant, or passionate. It helps infuse a heightened sense of soul into everyday thought, word, and deed and reflects the movement of Divine Energy in our lives.

The roots of sacred dance are prehistoric and shrouded in mystery. From time immemorial, movement and dance have reflected the visceral connection felt between humans and the Sacred Source of life and consciousness. The experience of living incarnate in a physical body, upon the body of the earth, and within the body of Spirit is universally expressed through movement and dance.

Even in the paintings and sculptures in which the ancients depict their bodies, we can see clues about their internal attitudes and beliefs. Mimicry of ancient and traditional body images and movement can sometimes evoke emotions and strengths that help us in our lives today. I have been inspired by Egyptian and Mayan carvings of hand positions and regal postures to incorporate ancient gestures in my spiritual practice.

*Carmen Granados*

Playing with movement can help us learn new qualitative life lessons. For instance, a woman who had attended a workshop of mine some time ago shared an interesting story with me about her experience with learning flamenco dancing. Somewhat timid by nature, she had been working for a large corporation for many years, and it was time for her to ask for a raise. She found that the strong, confident outward posture of the flamenco dancers helped her summon the inner strength and energy she needed to get what she deserved and practiced the flamenco posture in the ladies' room before going to meet with her boss. She got her raise.

The following pages present a brief history of the rich interplay of dance as a spiritual expression of virtually every region of the world, together with some short meditations and meditative exercises that will help you get used to a new repertoire of body-mind movements.


# ANCIENT TIMES

In some of the oldest cave drawings, human beings are shown with the animals they hunted in scenes that seem to reflect the Great Dance of Life. In depicting the animals of their world, prehistoric artists would invoke the strength of the bull, the speed of the stag, the transformational power of the snake. Egyptian carvings depict temple dancers moving in devotional praise to their gods. In the Old Testament, the prophet Miriam, in Exodus 15:20, led the people in a dance of thanksgiving when the Jews were freed from Pharaoh and found safe passage across the Red Sea. She took a timbrel (a hand drum similar to a tambourine) in her hand, "and all the women went out after her with timbrels and with dances."

In Aramaic, the language of the common people in the Middle East until the middle of the nineteenth century, the word for "rejoice" and "dance" is the same. The Jews, for instance, have always been a dancing people, with a long history of community dancing to celebrate births and weddings, bar and bas mitzvahs, and other holiday events. According to Dr. Doug Adams, professor emeritus at the Pacific School of Religion in Berkeley, California, families used dancing to express hospitality to their guests, saying, in essence, "We are glad you are here. It is an event worthy of celebrating. Call the musicians. Call out our friends so we can dance together."

A major theme of the community dances was the underlying understanding that when a community dances in one circle, they are enacting their connection to one another and to the One God. The circle was a physical symbol of an ancient Kabbalistic understanding of God as Holy Source of Oneness. A large part of Jewish sacred dance involved inviting the community to acknowledge its unity and its traditions with ancestral dances. As we'll see in other dancing cultures, the sacred circle of the community and reverence for the ancestors are common themes. The songs and dances of the Jews carried on traditions and beliefs of their ancestors and communicated them from generation to generation.

Throughout the Old Testament, the souls of individual dancers are said to move them into spontaneous expressions of gratitude, sorrow, joy, grief, and hopes for the future. In Ecclesiastes 3:4 dance is listed as one of the many experiences of a lifetime ("A time to weep and a time to laugh; a time to mourn and a time to dance"), while in Psalms 149:3 dance is seen as a vehicle for worship ("Let them praise His name in the dance"). Jewish influence on dance and culture spread throughout the Middle East and Europe as a result of the diaspora of the Babylonian captivity, in which the Jewish people were taken from their homeland and dispersed widely.

However, after the unsuccessful Jewish rebellions against the Romans in the first and second centuries A.D., Roman oppression increased, and the general pall that descended over the Jewish communities included the abandonment of joyful rituals, including sacred dance. This situation persisted for centuries. Murray Silberling, in his book *Dancing for Joy*, notes that ecstatic sacred dance finally returned to Judaism as a result of Hasidism, a revivalist movement that sprang up in Poland early in the eighteenth century C.E. Hasidism gradually influenced the return of dance to other Orthodox Jewish sects as well, and today Hasidic Jews still celebrate the Shabbat with joyful dance.

Cultures that dance are tuned in to "the spark of the infinite that energizes each of us," as Gabrielle Roth writes in *Maps to Ecstasy*, "hence, freeing the spirit means fanning that spark of infinity into a present-day flame, channeling the energy of the ultimate into the now, embodying the eternal in our finite lives."

## THE BLURRING OF FORMS— SPAIN AND NORTH AFRICA

The roots of ethnic and sacred dance forms often blend into each other. For instance, the Gypsy roots of flamenco run back through Moorish culture to North Africa. The castanets used by the Gypsies developed from the finger cymbals played by the Moorish dancers and before them by Egyptian temple dancers. We also see Egyptian dancers using wooden clacking sticks, related to throwing sticks dating back to 3000 B.C. The delicate sounds of the tiny cymbals and sharp rhythmic sounds of the clacking sticks reminded participants of the spiritual intention of the dance. We have, then, finger cymbals and clacking sticks evolving into castanets, and Egyptian and North African dance moving into Spain and evolving into flamenco.

Sounds and movements in virtually every religion are used as powerful calls to attention, drawing us to the present and centering us in the sacred moment. My husband and I recently attended a beautiful flamenco church service in which the castanets and the commanding strength of the flamenco dances served as powerful instruments for directing the spiritual focus of all worshipers. The flamenco dances were incorporated into hymns and scriptural readings. Percussive sounds are used to catalyze mindfulness in many Eastern and indigenous traditions that use cymbals, bells, gongs, Tibetan singing bowls, chimes, and percussion of all types. African and Native American rituals and dances use the drum and rattle, with the rhythmic beat inducing an altered state of consciousness and a spiritual connection.

Routes of trade over time helped to carry many of the cultural traditions of the world to new audiences. The sacred sounds, instruments, and dances blended with the traditions of their new homelands and became something unique to the new communities in which they flourished. Belly dancing, for instance, developed and spread in this manner. The dance probably began in the Middle East as a nomadic tribal dance and spread southwest into North Africa and northwest into the Balkans and Eastern Europe. Middle Eastern, North African, and Gypsy variations all exist today. Some modern dancers prefer the older term *oriental dance*, feeling that *belly dance* is a pejorative term, more descriptive of the traditional costume than of the dance itself.

*Aywah! Ethnic Dance Company*

Dance historians believe that belly dancing may have evolved from a ritual that prepared young pubescent girls for childbearing. Belly dancing also may have served as a spiritual initiation into the mysteries of a uniquely feminine path to divine connection, which, in many prehistoric centuries, centered around a Great Goddess. Originally, the women entrusted with the knowledge of this dance would have performed it only for other women. Men would have been excluded. In fact, I asked a friend of mine, who has studied tribal belly dance for many years, if she had the opportunity to dance while she was visiting with relatives in Saudi Arabia recently. She replied, "Oh, yes. Every night after dinner in the kitchen with the women."

To me the fluidity of the movements of the spine and arms that are used in belly dancing represents important qualities that we need to develop in our daily lives: resilience, adaptation, and flexibility. When we play with this movement in workshops, the participants usually discover one of two feelings: some will feel that the sinuousness of the movement releases energy and frees them in places in their lives where they feel stuck; others will feel more sensual or sexual. Of course, you may find something altogether different in your own exploration.

# AFRICA AND THE AFRICAN DIASPORA

Africa is home to a wealth of sacred dances, many of which celebrate the community, its ceremonies marking life's passages, and its connections to nature and to one another. Very often each dance has a specific rhythm with steps known to everyone in the community, who usually dance together. The dance and the rhythms often have a global meaning to the participants, even though the separate steps and gestures don't necessarily convey a specific idea. For example, the drummers use the *mandjiani* rhythm to announce that a celebration is at hand. "Come and dance mandjiani to participate in our celebration." The *focodoba* and other rhythms call the community to different dances that mark weddings, puberty rituals, naming ceremonies, the harvest, or funerals, reinforcing the unity among the members of the community.

The sounds accompanying African dances range from the use of the human voice alone to percussion and wind orchestras. Masai tradition uses vocal music primarily, because the sparse landscape in which the Masai dwell offers few trees and animals from which to craft drums. On the other hand, West Africans often use large collections of instruments, with the musicians following as many as five or more different rhythmic beats simultaneously. The result is a polyrhythmic pattern considerably more complex than music in which each drummer simply plays a variation of a specific rhythm. It's analogous to trying to dance to an orchestra in which half the musicians are playing a waltz and the rest a tango. Experienced dancers coordinate the movements of different parts of their bodies with the various rhythms. The head may move to one rhythm, the arms to another, and the feet to still a third.

*The Harambee Dance Ensemble*

Differences in cultural consciousness show up in dance forms. Many movements in African dance, for instance, project horizontally along the plane of the earth. This symbolizes that our grounding, our connection to the earth, lets us also connect with Spirit as Life Force. Jumps emphasize the landing, the return of the dancer to rootedness. This contrasts with Western ballet—with its jumps, lifts, leaps, and upward reaches—all seeking a heaven or an ecstatic sphere that does not exist here on earth. Other African dance forms use an undulating motion, reflecting in some dances the motion of the sea and in others the motion of a snake. The snake is a positive image in African tradition and also represents the Life Force, or God force, in the world.

Sacredness is defined by the quality of intention we bring to any and all acts of living. Recently, my husband and I dined with another couple who had lived in various parts of Africa for several years. The husband told me that he hadn't seen any sacred dances in Africa—"just a bunch of fertility rites." Yet to me, and to many indigenous people, these rites *are* sacred. If you see sex as a sacred and holy part of the Life Force or an immanent God, then fertility and sexuality are holy. Sacredness can exist in the recognition of a young girl's menarche or in a dance of celebration for the coming of the rains.

The dances and rituals of many African nations are imbued with reverence for the ancestors, not only those of an individual's direct ancestral line but the ancestral connections of the entire community. Gail Thompson, with whom I studied African dance for several years, would often tell us, "The ancestors gave us life. They passed us the wisdom of evolution. They suffered and endured to extend to us this precious Life Force." From the African viewpoint they continue to guide us, give us information, and give us "what for" when we deserve it. They serve not only as our connection to the "other side" but also as our connection to the earth and our rightful place within it. The dancer of a community ritual becomes immersed in the richer meaning of the dance because it is basically the same dance that his or her ancestors carried forward from past generations. The movements and rhythms of the dance become a powerful connection to the ancestors.

The African ritual of ancestor worship does not seem particularly esoteric when we consider the Roman Catholic practice of canonization of ancestors. Both traditions honor the spiritual attainment and wisdom of the ancestors and create a process by which they will always be remembered and can be called upon by future generations for guidance.

The Americas have a wide variety of African dances brought west by the slaves. Most have been altered from their original forms since their practice was often prevented or impeded by the cruel lives the Africans endured in the American colonies. Kidnapped from their homelands, slaves were deliberately separated from friends, families, and other village members when they arrived in the Americas to break their spirits. They were placed with other abductees whose language and culture were different to minimize their ability to plan for mutiny or escape. Many communities also banned slaves from gathering together in celebration and dancing, out of the fear that during these gatherings the slaves could plot to revolt. Nonetheless, the captured slaves remembered and preserved what they could from their original homelands, often dancing surreptitiously in small groups in their quarters. Their legacy is a rich amalgamation of rhythm and dance, which includes, to name a small handful, calypso, Haitian dance, the Brazilian capoeira, samba, batuque, and the rituals of Macumba.

I recently took a West African dance workshop with a teacher who explained the emphasis on pelvic motion seen in many African-based Caribbean dances, which is different from purely African dances. This change in form occurred during the ship voyage, when the slaves were transported to the islands. Chains clamped to each arm and leg restrained them. Their torsos were all they could move for exercise, and the origins for the calypso and samba were born from their confinement. When the African slaves were finally let out of the chains and could dance, they developed dances that combined pronounced pelvic motions with explosive arm and leg movements and signified bursts of physical exuberance, the desire for freedom, and the vitality of a people denied their own lives.


Each of us will find different internal experiences when we try movement from different traditions. One woman told me that the African dance elements in my classes helped her gain access to a "wild woman" energy in her, a naturally passionate and exuberant part of her being that resisted the deadening influence of an imprisoning daily routine. Many of us could use a little of this energy to jolt us out of the habitual patterns into which we settle in response to the everyday demands of life.

If I had to choose only one word to describe African dance, it would unquestionably be *joy*. I'll share a piece of a dance with you here that combines several themes that are seen in a lot of African dances. The movement expresses gratitude for the earth, for all our relationships here, and to the "Unseen" for our ancestors and spirit guides.

## ∼ The Shimmy of Gratitude ∼

*Begin standing with feet hip-width apart, arms at your sides, palms down. Inhale and exhale deeply eight times, sending cleansing breaths through your body and feeling the earth beneath your feet. Bend your knees slightly, creating "soft knees," a position that's easier on your lower back than standing rigidly with straight legs. Place your hands on the front of your thighs, then lift your hands about eight inches from your body, fingertips pointing down toward the earth. Bend slightly at the waist if your back allows this movement comfortably. Let your gaze follow your hands. With small movements, press your right shoulder forward, then your left shoulder forward. When you feel comfortable with the position and the movement, increase your tempo. This creates a shimmy. Listening to African drum music during this moving prayer adds joy, focus, and exuberance to the movement.*

*As you do this shimmy, think of everything the earth provides for you and for which you are grateful. Imagine that you are sending the energy of your gratitude out from your fingertips to the earth. Continue to shimmy and bring your hands up from the earth to your heart level. Think of all the relationships that hold meaning for you and for which you are grateful. Send your gratitude to those people for their presence in your life. Continue the shimmy and bring your hands back above your head in honor of those who are no longer in the physical world. Honor your ancestors, guides, and the spiritual realms. Hold your hands still for a moment as you finish. Amen.*

Some Caribbean dances—such as calypso, nago, and yanwalu—contain steps in which the dancers pivot all their movement around one stationary foot. This step also goes back to times when slaves on the plantations were made to wear one leg iron at all times of the day and during all activities to prevent their escape. While enduring this abominable oppression, however, the Africans rose above their dismal circumstances and allowed their souls to dance to their spirit guides, developing their own unique dances and steps. They danced in their own secret places that can never be captured, and preserved the enormity of their own inner spirit, sustaining hope for a better future for themselves and their families.

Here is a step from the calypso tradition. As you perform it, allow yourself to ask your own spirit the following questions: Is there a place in my life in which I am feeling physically or emotionally stuck or trapped? Is there anything I can do to change this trap into an experience of freedom? If I cannot change the physical specifics of this situation, what can I learn here and now from it? What qualities of heart can I bring to bear on the situation? How will I turn this situation into my own wisdom tradition?

## ~ Calypso Liberation ~

*Begin by standing in the middle of a room, so that you have enough space around you to move. Stand comfortably, feet shoulder-width apart so that you are balanced with your weight evenly distributed on both legs. Let your arms hang to the side. Breathe out and in slowly three times, becoming aware of your entire body, from the top of your head to your toes. Feel the energy circulating through your legs. With the left foot planted firmly on the ground, pivot around it with the right leg, in a clockwise motion, moving backward in small steps. Think of a compass making a perfect circle. As you turn, place your left hand over your heart while you extend your right arm palm up, hold, and ask the questions. Complete one revolution, then switch to a counterclockwise motion, changing feet, keeping the right foot planted on the ground while you pivot with the left foot. While you ask yourself the questions, remember that often questions are easier to ask than answers are to find. That's okay. Once you release your questions to the world, you have opened yourself up to receive the answers, which often follow this exercise.*

The undulating rhythm of African dance also occurs in Haitian dance, which I began to study in San Francisco in the mid-1990s with Blanche Brown, who had immersed herself in the culture and spirit of Haiti and was initiated into the traditional religion. Blanche choreographs and directs her own Haitian dance company, Petit La Croix. One day when we were discussing a sacred aspect of Haitian dance, specifically the undulating rhythm of yanwalu, she quoted her mentor, her "spiritual godfather," who told her, "Your dance is how you pray." That powerful statement is a great definition of sacred dance and embodied prayer.

The rhythm known as yanwalu, which Blanche and I had been discussing, is often used to call forth the Loa, or spirits. Danballah is the oldest and wisest Loa in Haitian tradition and is represented in the form of a serpent, which symbolizes the Life Force in all its glory, as in Africa. The serpent is analogous to the God force—the force within us, within all beings, within all things. It is within us, and we are all within it as well. The Life Force contains and interconnects us. Unlike many Western religious traditions, which see God as transcendent, as being a higher force outside of us and beyond our individual reach, the Haitian viewpoint recognizes the force as immanent, inherent in all things. The Haitian dancer embraces the essence of the serpent by sending a rhythmic rolling motion through the spine that undulates into the extremities, neck, and head. With subtle variations, Haitian dance also uses an undulating movement to honor and call forth the Loa (gods) of the oceans.

We will be using this undulating chest and torso movement in several dances that appear later in this book. To me the movement evokes a sense of waking up the heart and pulsing my intention along with the heartbeat. See what it brings up for you as you try following the steps.

## ∾ Danballah's Blessing ∾

*Begin standing with your feet shoulder-width apart. Take a few deep, cleansing breaths and let your knees "soften" a bit. The basic movement is simple and combines thought with action. Imagine that there's a string attached to the center of your chest. Let the string pull up your chest. Now resist the string and allow your chest to fall. This may cause your chest and upper back to cave in a bit. Next, bend your elbows and bring your hands, palms up, to the sides of your shoulders, to evoke a feeling of receiving a blessing. Repeat the movement until it feels natural to you. At that point you might want to add some Afro-Haitian drum music and experiment with different rhythms.*

*Blanche Brown describes the "rise and fall" as a rolling motion that*

*originates deep in the spine and travels out into the arms. Try to even out the rise and fall of your movements so that you get the sense of the rolling rhythm that ripples through you and out of you. Allow the sense of receiving and sending blessings to roll through your inner awareness as well as your body, transforming your movement into an embodied prayer.*

The energy of Danballah and yanwalu seems similar to the concept of kundalini energy in Tantric yoga. The kundalini is the energy of consciousness. In most of us it lies dormant. The feminine form of this energy resides at the base of the spine, coiled in the first chakra, or energy center, like a sleeping serpent. With proper spiritual practice, which includes focused meditation, this energy can be awakened so that it uncoils and ascends up the spine (another serpentlike shape) through each of seven principal chakras, or energy centers, that lie along the spine. When it arrives at the seventh, or crown, chakra at the top of the head, it unites with the energy of Shiva, the male principle of energy, which is the consciousness of the Universe. This union yields enlightenment, and the individual attains a state of *samadhi*, or bliss and unity with all that is. Similarly, summoning the Loas through dance connects us with the greater energy of the Universe so that we can transcend our individual situations and awaken to greater Oneness of Spirit.

# BRAZIL

The roots of the rich African cultures were transplanted throughout the Western Hemisphere, growing into dance forms specific to the places in which they grew and flowered. In Brazil the African semba became the samba, and the batuque evolved as well. Both the samba and the batuque rely heavily on the umbigada, a sensual pelvic salute, when two dancers touch navel to navel to signal the changing of partners.

The roots of the samba celebrate creation and reflect an inherent gratitude for the gift of energy, the sacred Life Force in each of us. The rolling torso and shimmy of the shoulders and arms are reminders to live with an open heart. A teacher of mine once said that a person with a closed heart can never learn to samba.

The shimmying pelvic movements of the samba evoke the phrase "Shake it loose." What is it you want to "shake loose" in your own life? A middle-aged man from one of my workshops found that the samba shook up his world. The vibrancy and loose freedom of the dances helped him become aware of how he inhibited himself from taking risks in other areas of his life. The ebullience he felt dancing led him to want to feel this same energy in his financial and personal life. Within two years of his finding his own dancing spirit, he left the stifling corporate world in which he had spent twenty years to start his own business and married for the first time at age fifty-three! Although you may not want to shake it up that much, samba will definitely give you the energy to put your own spirit in action.

Learning to shimmy—to free yourself—is not difficult. Beginners often get confused by trying to shimmy from the chest, when the movement originates in the shoulder blades of the upper back. This shimmy is different from the one you did in The Shimmy of Gratitude. In that one you focused on sending the energy of gratitude through your arms and out through your fingertips. In this one you will concentrate on shimmying from the core of your body, your upper spine, to wake yourself up and remain receptive and open in your heart.

## ⌣ The Shimmy of an Open Heart ⌣

*To shimmy, pull your right shoulder blade back and then release it. Repeat with your left shoulder blade. When you feel comfortable with the movement, quicken the pace as you alternate shoulders. Keep your head and neck still. Open your arms to the sides, elbows bent slightly, with your hands at the level of your shoulders or a little lower, palms up. Lift your chest as you continue to shimmy. This encourages the feeling of an open, receptive heart.*

The African dances of Angola became the Brazilian capoeira, which combines drum rhythms, dance, and fighting movements. The capoeira looks like a lyrical dance but is in fact a fierce martial art.

Three elements contributed heavily to the Brazilian culture of today—the ancient dance of ceremonial healing of the indigenous people, the African culture of the slaves, and the Roman Catholicism of the Portuguese. The Afro-Brazilian religion of Macumba grew out of this amalgamation, along with its sects, Candomble and Umbanda. The rituals of these religions express complex emotions, often including the need for physical healing of the participants.

In a Brazilian dance class, I learned an embodied prayer of self-healing that comes out of the Macumba tradition. With hands clenched tight, the dancer mimics the rhythm of beating drums by hitting the afflicted place on his body. The dancer contorts to show the ugliness of the agony, whether it be physical or emotional. The dance gradually increases in speed and intensity, culminating with expansive, open gestures. The arms whip and the hands flip at the wrist, symbolizing the release from illness or dysfunction.

This self-healing dance reminds me of the truths on which contemporary twelve-step programs are based: In order to heal yourself, you must first acknowledge and speak of your dysfunction or ailment. The dance recognizes that all of our spirits have a dark, shadow side, weaknesses, or injuries that we would prefer to ignore. We'd rather gloss over them than acknowledge and "dance them." As illustrated in the dances of Macumba, however, once we bring the dark side into the light and acknowledge it, we can work with it and ultimately release it. Amazingly, ancient rituals often antedate modern psychotherapeutic practices in earthy, effective, embodied ways. Macumba has had it right for centuries.

# NORTH AMERICAN NATIVES

On the North American continent, many dances of the indigenous Americans share similar themes, even though the cultural diversity of the nations is vast. Common threads include a profound reverence for the earth and the ancestors, and the conviction that we all are related to other living beings and the Universe as a whole, united in the Great Spirit.

Reflecting this unity, many dances are traditionally performed in a circle. The circle itself is a sacred symbol, symbolizing the whole of life. All living creatures are considered equal—the two-leggeds, the four-leggeds, the winged ones, the creeping and crawling ones, the plants, rocks, and trees—all are part of the Earth Mother herself.

Some indigenous cultures, such as the Canadian Plains Indians and some of the native Middle Eastern tribes, don't even have a specific word for music or dance, because these arts are intrinsic to the very fabric of living—they cannot be separated out. Just as we assume that if we are alive, we breathe, so in some Native American cultures, if you are alive, you dance. What a full, rich definition of being, so much more exciting and vibrant and fully, humanly engaged than "I think, therefore I am."

For centuries the sacred ceremonies, their music, and dance were individual expressions of the tribes and their clans. The ceremonies transmitted the tribes' individual history and stories from one generation to the next, promoting the unity and interdependence of the community. With the coming of the white man, some of the tribes lost their sovereignty and were banished to intertribal reservations, where Christian religious customs were imposed upon them and obscured the old ways.

Because of the close proximity of the various tribes, however, intertribal dances developed, and the individual tribal distinctions of the dances became blurred. After World War I, Native Americans began to hold what was called a pow-I-u, a ceremony and picnic to honor the returning Native American veterans from that war. These celebrations included the intertribal dances that have evolved into the modern powwow. Traditionally celebrated as a victory dance for Native American warriors, the modern powwow celebrates the triumph of traditional values over the complexities of the modern world.

The intricate, colorful costumes and the rich sounds of rattles, drums, and bells in a modern powwow can give us only a rough idea of the many and varied traditional Native American ceremonial dances and their deeper significance. For example, the women's fancy shawl dance comes from a deep process of grieving the death of a lost warrior or loved one. In the history of the Plains Indians, the shawl dance symbolizes the butterfly in flight. Originally, the symbolic forming of a chrysalis by the grieving widow preceded the colorful dance. The bereaved wraps a large blanket around herself and lies in a fetal position facedown on the floor, wrapped inside her grief. She is free to feel her pain fully for as long as she needs. When she has completed this inward, self-contained stage, she rises out of the cocoon, as does the butterfly. The shawl dance symbolizes that she is now free to begin a new life. As with Macumba, the true origins of this dance reveal a psychoemotional healing process of great wisdom. Its message can even be seen in Martha Graham's great 1931 solo *Lamentation*, in which she sits on a bench, her body enclosed in fabric that she manipulates and stretches from head to toe.

The body records our personal histories. Love, joy, grief, and pain are all "written on the body." Sacred dance and embodied prayer help us express and resolve deep emotions so that the body, mind, and spirit are in sync. For instance, moving in ways that are open, strong, and expressive can be very healing to a person whose nature and ordinary body language are shy and retiring.

Another well-known dance on the modern powwow circuit is the "sneak up," a celebration of the hunt, in which the dancers are bent over low to the earth as if they were sneaking up on their prey. This tribal dance also illustrates the importance of standing your ground with commitment and acting in unity for the good of the community.

I recently met Maggie Blackettle, a Native American Blackfoot, who is more than eighty years old and still leads her family in the largest powwow in Coeur d'Alene, Idaho. When she was interviewed in the local newspaper, she told the reporter, "It's not the competition that matters, [but] the dancing prayers that keep me going."

The following ritual movement, which I developed in honor of the wisdom in traditional Native American prayer, is excellent for grounding yourself and for connecting to the earth, especially if you've been in the concrete maze of a city for too long. The movement accompanies the following Native American prayer: "Beauty before me, beauty behind me, beauty below me, beauty all around, beauty above me, beauty am I." This prayer puts us in touch with the beauty of creation wherever we cast our gaze and reminds us that we are an integral part of the circle. With this affirmation held within you, think of how you can make your actions reflect this beauty today. You might want to listen to a tape of Native American flute or drumming music as you perform the following steps.

## ∽ The Beauty Prayer ∽

*Begin standing in the center of the room with feet hip-width apart, arms hanging loosely at your sides. Inhale and exhale, slowly and deeply. As you perform the following steps, let your feet connect with the earth in reverence. Begin by slowly walking in place. If you are listening to a tape, step to the rhythm in the music. With palms down at waist level or lower, begin to pulse your hands (as if you were doing a very abbreviated basketball dribble), sensing the energy of the earth. Let your steps and your gaze pick up the direction of the prayer. If you want to synchronize your movements to particular phrases of the prayer, try the following:*

*As you say the words "Beauty before me," take four steps forward with arms extended in front of you, palms out, as if sensing the wonders of the world within your grasp. As you say "beauty behind me," take four steps back with palms lowered and pressing behind. When you say "beauty below me," step in place with palms facing the earth at waist level. For "beauty all around me," turn 360 degrees with palms up at shoulder level. For "beauty above me," take four steps in place with your arms raised overhead, palms up toward the sky, fluttering your fingers as if your hands were treetops being rustled by the wind. And for the most important words of the prayer, "beauty am I," lower your arms slowly with your palms facing your body, finishing the prayer with crossed hands over your heart. Feel the energy of this embodied prayer move through you. With your feet firmly on the ground, you're connected to ancestral footsteps, ancestral strength, and love. Repeat this sequence five to ten times.*

How wonderful does it feel to express your own beauty while acknowledging the beauty of the world around you? The prayer is so simple but is one of the most effective in expressing joy and invoking optimism and the energy of gratitude and blessing. See whether you can take a regular few minutes of time out of your busy day to acknowledge the significance of beauty, within you and outside of you. Become one with the beauty of the circle of life: breathe in beauty.

# THE SOUTH SEA ISLANDS AND INDONESIA

The two major unifying themes of many world dances—reverence for all nature and the Life Force, and reverence for the ancestors—are also prominent in the island civilizations of the Pacific and Indian oceans. The sacred circle of ceremonial dance is often seen there as well.

A distinctive feature of Polynesian and South Sea Island dances is that many of the individual movements and gestures have a specific meaning known to onlookers and dancers alike. The dances usually tell stories that emerge from the sign language of the dancer's movements, keep the histories intact, and evoke the deep spiritual connection to the Sacred Source. This is different from other cultures, in which the montage of the dance as a whole evokes an emotional response from the community.

The graceful swaying motions seen in Polynesian dances evoke for me the energy of the earth and the heart. In the following exercise, you can experiment with this energy for yourself.

## ～ Sings My Soul to Creation ～

*Clear a space that allows you about four feet of movement in all directions. Begin standing, with your feet hip-width apart. Let your arms relax by your sides. Take a few deep, slow, cleansing breaths to bring creative energy through your body. Feel where you are in the room, then begin by stepping your right foot to the right, then bring your left foot to meet it, feet together. Step right again; step together close with your left foot. Then reverse the movement to the left side. Step left with your left foot; bring the right foot to meet it. Again step left; step together with your right foot. That will bring you back to your starting position.*

Next you'll add gentle hip movements. Most people think incorrectly that the graceful swaying of the hips in hula comes from pushing the hips to the side, but it actually comes from bending the knees during the movement. By lowering your center of gravity, you allow the pelvis to move parallel with the plane of the ground, connecting with the energy of the earth. The "soft knees" release your lower back and hips to sway quite naturally, as if you were a bamboo tree swaying in the wind but always returning to your starting position.

Next you'll add some hand movements. Raise your arms in front of you, palms up, at the level of the heart. Extend your arms out 45 degrees to your sides to signify your gratitude for the beauty of the natural world. Then bring one hand palm up to the level of the heart, and let your right hand figuratively pick up some of your heart energy from your left hand, bringing it to your mouth and then up to the sky. This movement embodies a creation prayer: "Sings my soul to your beauty." I like to repeat this ten to twenty times, several repetitions to each of the four directions. The power of this exercise is even stronger in a beautiful natural setting.

Hula is currently popular among young Japanese women, who travel to Hawaii for lessons and sometimes compete in the King Kamehameha competition, one of the competitive hula world's major events. Some of these women are even learning a traditional form of hula known as kahiko, which historically is danced for indigenous gods and involves chanting in Hawaiian.

In some of the island cultures, the arts themselves are considered a spiritual practice. Margaret Mead once said, "Everyone is an artist in Bali." The Balinese encourage artistic endeavors from early childhood—dancing, painting, playing music, creating batik, sculpting wood, performing with theater puppets—the specific form doesn't matter. Everyone engages in some sort of creation of beauty because this pursuit is seen as integral to connecting with Spirit and expressing the primal energy of creation.

The arts of Bali are strongly intertwined with the island's religious life. Most ceremonies include some kind of physical display to attract the gods and to delight the inhabitants. In a recent article in the *New York Times*, Dr. Anak Agung Made Djelantik, a physician-prince from the eastern regency of Karangasem, who lectures on aesthetics at the College of Indonesian Arts in Denpasar, said, "The arts are an invitation for the gods to come down and join the people. There is a very physical contact with the unseen, with the ancestors . . .

*Balinese Mask Dance*

which makes the people in the village very happy. That is why the arts will never go away."

The arts of Bali have also been transported to other cultures. For example, Balinese influences can be seen in the contemporary music of American composers Philip Glass and Lou Harrison and in the puppetry of Julie Taymor, who designed the Broadway show *The Lion King*.

## THE ROLE OF TRANCE

Many world cultures practice ceremonies that include trance and mysticism. Altered states of consciousness, though very common in everyday life throughout the world, seem strange to Westerners when they are deliberately induced as part of worship. The trance state can be experienced by the individual dancer or by members of the same group who share a common vision. Dance rituals can also actively take the dancer into a trance state. A good example of this is the whirling dervish dance of the Sufis. The spiraling dance itself is the vehicle that takes the dancer into the deep awareness of the quiet center within us. At other times initiates enter into the deep trance state first and are then able to physically demonstrate unusual or paranormal activities through the dance or embodied ritual.

My husband, Brad, attended a Buddhist fire-walking ceremony in Japan. As the blazing logs burned down to form a bed of hot coals sixty feet long, which would take more than an hour and a half, the monks who would perform the embodied ritual sat on the ground in meditative poses, gently swaying and chanting. Those who had come to observe stood at respectful distances around the ceremonial area, but the monks seemed unaware of them. Eventually, as dusk was falling, the monks stood, one by one, and slowly walked across the length of red-hot coals in their bare feet. As they slowly walked, they chanted while holding their hands clasped in attitudes of prayer. They communicated with the essential nature of all things. This embodied prayer state demonstrates the great mystery of our possibilities when we expand our awareness beyond limited thinking.

I witnessed a similar ceremony when I traveled with a group of friends to Fiji, and we were invited to attend a fire-walking ritual. The Fijian men participating in the ritual were to communicate the needs of their tribe to the Fijian gods. My friends and I were expecting to witness the same kind of intense, focused, reverential prewalk preparation that Brad had witnessed in Japan. We were surprised when the men casually strolled onto the hot coals and sat down. They spoke among themselves for five to ten minutes before standing and finishing the walk.

The men, who had learned to enter a deep trance, performed the embodied prayer in an astonishingly unpretentious manner. Had they not been in an altered state, they would not have been able to perform the ritual unharmed. Trances, or altered states of consciousness, are natural and common in this culture. Little pomp and fanfare are required or expected in their manifestation. The men who performed the ritual were able to split their conscious attention so that one part remained in a deep trance while the other part was engaged in conversation. The Fijian men could maintain a double state of awareness that allowed the paranormal feat.

The Balinese have a cultural heritage of trance dances. In one of the sanghyang dances, two girls, who are supposedly untrained in the dance's intricate choreography, go into a trance and, eyes firmly shut, move in perfect unison. The dance is named after the Divine Spirit that inhabits them.

Elsewhere in Indonesia I've witnessed a trance dance called the Kriss dance, in which men dance themselves into an altered state of consciousness. Each man allows himself to become possessed by a spirit that makes him turn a viciously pointed, curved knife on himself. He repeatedly and forcefully jabs the knife into his abdomen, but it does not penetrate the skin. Not even a scratch appears during this frenzied and chaotic dance. In this culture, the idea of possession is not feared. Spirit honors the dancer by allowing this deep and intimate form of communion with it. The goal of dances like the Kriss dance, or the embodied ritual of fire walking, is not the paranormal expression itself. Trance is a mind-set of communion with a Greater Energy that teaches us that our lives are unequivocally part of a greater reality.

In Australia Aboriginal dance ceremonies rely heavily on altered states. Dreamtime trances recall the mythology of a culture thought to be at least forty thousand years old. *Dreamtime* is the name given to the world of primordial energy and is the source of inner wisdom and knowledge. Within the Dreamtime are totem figures that provide humans with an immortal identity that continues from the beginning of time, until now, and on into the future. This identity allows the believer to contact the ancestors, the wisdom, and the mythic beings that reside in the world of the Dreamtime.

The Rainbow Serpent is one of their most revered mythological figures, and some believe that it is through this creature that all life arose. The spiritual dances and rituals of the Aborigines induce a deep, altered state of awareness from which many individuals are able to gain paranormal abilities. The Aboriginal culture was probably one of the first to learn how to alter consciousness and use this state as a routine cultural activity throughout the community. In other cultures of both the East and West, ritual access to these states was largely reserved for priests, shamans, or other adepts, though these spiritual leaders might include members of the community or congregation in some of the rituals.

## THE FAR EAST AND INDIA

Spiritual dance styles for storytelling are common throughout the Far East and include Thai, Cambodian, and Indian dancing. Noh, the classic theater of Japan, contains elements of dance. All these forms are highly stylized. The characters and plot change very little. As in South Sea Island dances, each subtle gesture or posture usually means something very specific and scripted. Even the direction in which the dancer's eyes look can change the identity of the character or deity that is being represented. In classical Indian dances, dozens of different specific positions of the eyes, head, and hands are combined to convey innumerable emotional nuances. Everyone in the community learns the stories of these dance dramas by heart from childhood. Seeing them performed over and over again preserves the community's history, spiritual outlook, and cultural lessons.

These dances are helpful for tapping into the world of archetypal spiritual energies. In the angular, grounded images of an ancient, mythic warrior, you can find the centeredness from which you need to address or bear up under some challenge today. Nataraj, who is Shiva in his aspect as the Hindu Lord of the Dance, is often depicted standing on one leg, crushing a dwarf, which represents ignorance. I find it empowering to imitate Nataraj's classical pose when I need to make proper decisions and stand by my convictions. Kuan-Yin, a female deity recognized throughout much of Chinese-influenced Asia, represents compassion and peace. Her beautiful countenance is often expressed as a standing figure, holding a lotus flower near her heart in her left hand, as her right hand extends a blessing to all beings. I often mimic Kuan-Yin's posture when I meditate to remind myself that I, too, may extend compassion and blessings to all beings.

Such gestures and postures hold the wisdom of thousands of years of human understanding. By experimenting with posture and movement, you can consciously evoke a powerful internal energy that can change your life.

*Indian (Bharatanatyam), Abhinaya School of Dance*

Buddhist traditions contribute internal movement and a heightened consciousness to some Eastern dance traditions. A dancer's own meditative focus is also believed to raise the vibrational energy of the observer's consciousness, bestowing blessings of enlightenment on spectator and dancer alike. Bells, bowls, chants, and other auditory devices of Buddhism are used to awaken the mind to the present moment, since only in the present can we experience oneness. Many of the Eastern moving arts, such as tai chi and qi gong, share this internal quietude and grace as part of the moving practice.

The stylized dances of the East are often characterized by exquisitely slow, deliberate movement. For some Westerners, it is almost painful to watch, since we are used to being in constant motion. However, when you engage in a formal meditative dance, focusing your attention inside of the movements themselves, you concentrate your energy, calling it back from all the distractions of the day. You become grounded in the pure expression of each gesture and achieve the mind space from which excellence in action is born.

Here's a simple exercise to help you feel the difference between an externally motivated motion and one that comes from an internal focus.

## ～ External and Internal Focus of Movement ～

*Begin from a standing position with your hands relaxed at your sides. Now raise one arm out to your side to 90 degrees. Do this very, very slowly. Try to make the movement last at least sixty seconds. This movement is based on the external focus of moving your arm. Relax your arm and try it a second time and maintain this image in your mind as you do so: imagine that there is a large deflated balloon between your arm and your torso and that each time you exhale slowly, the balloon fills with a little air. As the balloon fills fuller, it naturally lifts your arm with it.*

Most people find the first part of the exercise very difficult. The body often wants to rebel and gets twitchy at the enforced control. In the second example your focus is helped by the visualization of the balloon, so that you're barely thinking about the movement itself. The movement becomes a natural outgrowth of your internal focus. It is not necessary to repeat this exercise once you understand the process. However, you can translate this awareness to a number of other slow exercise forms, such as tai chi or qi gong.

Another beautiful example of this slow, meditative movement is seen in the Japanese tea ceremony, in which a master prepares, serves, and shares cups of tea with the other participants. In an extraordinarily attentive manner, the tea master slowly makes each gesture and component part of the process an art form. The picking up of each utensil, the replacement of it when the master is finished with it, the pouring of the tea in a manner that allows the liquid to make music in the cup—all these things also capture the attention of the guests at the ceremony.

Whenever I am feeling scattered, with my thoughts going in a dozen directions at once, I borrow from these traditions of slow, attentive motion with the following physical meditation.

## ～ Body-Mind Focus—Slowing Down ～

*First, make yourself stop whatever you are doing and sit still for at least one minute. Then, begin to move purposely in slow motion. Allow the movement of only this moment to lead you to your next motion. Instead of aiming to walk across the room, for instance, focus on your heart and see whether it is being drawn somewhere, perhaps to a point across the room. Focusing inside, on the heart of the moment, allows the form of the movement to follow natu-*

*rally and slowly. In a very short time, this inner attention will clear your head and allow your spirit to engage in the activity of living once again.*

# BACK TO THE MIDDLE EAST— THE SUFIS

Sufism is a mystical practice of Islam. One Sufi order in particular, founded by the poet Rumi, uses internal meditative dance to connect with the Divine. Rumi was known as Mawlana, which means "teacher" or "master," and the order he founded is known as the Mawlawiyah order. Members of a Sufi fraternal order are known as dervishes, and the members of the Turkish Mawlawiyah order became known as whirling dervishes, because they spin about as they meditate and pray in a ritual called sema. The whirling movement of the dancer represents the activity of the outer world. The dancer is able to spin by focusing on the still point—the God point, which is stable and immutable—within the self. Although your entire body is moving, your center remains silent and still. While the body is engaged in active meditation, the spirit can be freed to connect with the Divine. These dances are wonderful metaphors as well as spiritual activities that remind us to stay centered and focused on the still point within ourselves no matter what circumstances of our lives may be swirling about us.

Other Sufi orders use very slow meditative movements, often combined with postures similar to advanced yogic postures that are rather difficult. The concentration necessary to accomplish the prescribed configuration of the body clears the mind of everyday thoughts. This focus and the repetitive nature of the movements induce a meditative, altered state of consciousness.

The following simple exercise comes from a Sufi tradition.

## ∼ Shifting Your State of Awareness ∼

*Begin by standing with your head facing front, then slowly turn your head to the right while shifting your eyes to the left. Reverse and turn your head left, shifting your eyes right. Repeat the movement six to eight times.*

It sounds easy, but this exercise is very difficult for most people. It is meant to disrupt the normal brain-body patterns of movement. Ordinarily, when we turn our head left, we are also looking toward that direction. Changing this pattern, which almost never happens naturally, causes a disruption of the nor-

63

mal brain pathways and is called a pattern interrupt. It is a way of waking up the brain from its habitual functioning. When we disrupt habitual brain functioning, we are more able to think in new ways and also alter our consciousness. Modern forms of clinical hypnotherapy use this same idea of a pattern interruption to introduce behavioral changes and psychological healing.

The following exercise, adapted from a Sufi group dance, illustrates the individual's connection to the larger community. It involves a traveling step, so clear a few feet of space around you before beginning.

### ∼ "I Am" Prayer for Connection ∼

*Stand with feet hip-width apart, arms hanging comfortably at your sides. Take a few deep, cleansing breaths, feeling the fresh air enter your lungs, while your feet are firmly connected to the earth. Begin by stepping forward lightly on the ball of your right foot, lean back on your left foot, then shift the weight back to your right foot. Repeat the pattern with your left foot. Each time you change your lead foot, you will be traveling forward on the step. Allow your body to enjoy the simplicity that accompanies this flexible movement. Once you are able to do this three-step pattern, you'll add two words to give deeper meaning to the exercise. On the first right step of the pattern, say "I." On the first left step, say "am." Allow yourself to travel in this walking meditation, feeling the resonance of the ancient chant, "I am." Repeat this traveling step for five to ten minutes.*

This simple dance movement is a living embodiment of the One Spirit, the Source of all things, and illustrates how, as in many of the great world religions, each person is an important link in the chain of being.

## CHRISTIANITY AND DANCE

Dance all of you. . . .
To the universe belongs the dancer.
—ACTS OF JOHN,
NEW TESTAMENT APOCRYPHA

As Christianity evolved, its rituals incorporated the culture of the lands in which it developed. The early Christian Church was made up primarily of

Jews and pagan tribal peoples from the Middle East and Southern Europe. These were dancing people. In the early church all the members danced in the sacred circle, much as all indigenous and tribal communities do now and have done for ages. In Europe, Celtic and other tribal traditions that dominated the culture of pre-Christian Europe for centuries also influenced Christian dance worship. Considering Christianity's roots, early Christian services could hardly have avoided using movement in the worship experience. In spite of treatises that denigrated the body by writers such as Origen in the second century and Saint Augustine in the fourth century, dancing as part of Christian worship persisted up to the time of the Protestant Reformation and even after that into the early 1800s.

Even though the body was considered a vehicle of sin, dancing in church was not seen as sinful. According to Dr. Doug Adams, world authority on early Christian worship, early services included circle dances that supported the notion that all members of the congregation were one in Christ. Processionals and dramatizations were also a popular part of the services. The very words *chorus* and *stanza* found in common hymnals are Latin for "dance" and "stand," respectively. These were choreographic directions for the congregation. Pews were not even introduced into churches until the early seventeenth century, and then only some nonstationary pews. Most could be moved to make room for the dances.

The dance in Christian worship included pageants, processions, circle dances, and folk dances. Some were practiced with great pomp and majesty, whereas others maintained the simplicity of their folk roots.

*Boston Liturgical Dance Ensemble*

Changes in dance forms over the centuries reflected the changes in the structure of the Roman Catholic Church. From the fourth century on, the church leadership became less egalitarian and more hierarchical in its structure, and by the ninth century, dance reflected these changes within the church structure. Between the ninth and fourteenth centuries, the structure of church dances gradually changed. Gone was the symbol of egalitarian participation, the simple sacred circle, replaced by a ceremonial form in which the bishops danced only with other bishops, the priests with other priests, and the congregation members with one another.

Finally, with the Reformation, dance was eliminated as part of the sacred experience in Protestant churches and persisted only in rudimentary ritualistic forms in Catholic services, such as kneeling, standing, and making the sign of the cross.

Even today some mainstream Christian churches are uncomfortable with even the simplest liturgical dances, as they are called, as part of the service, although dance is helpful for emphasizing a teaching, enlivening the worship service, and inspiring a deeper faith experience in the congregation. These liturgical dances might be used to dramatize a scriptural passage or to add to the celebratory atmosphere of a holy day or simply be hand gestures added to the singing of hymns. Nevertheless, sacred dance has returned to all sorts of Christian churches today as part of services of worship, both as inspirational performance and as an expression of spirituality in which the entire congregation can participate.

To illustrate the relationship between sacred dance and Christianity, I have adapted an embodied meditation from *The Healing Path of Prayer*, by Ron Roth. Here the cross is seen as a symbol of the power of Spirit in the world rather than as a symbol of death and sacrifice.

## ∽ The Heart of the Cross ∽

*Begin by standing in place with your feet together and your arms hanging comfortably at your sides. Feel the stillness within you for a few more seconds. Begin to breathe slowly and deeply, bringing your awareness to the crown of your head. Imagine that you can feel the energy of Spirit entering through the crown of your head and traveling down through your body, out through your feet, and into the earth. The vertical part of the cross symbolizes Spirit penetrating matter, waiting to be expressed in the world through you. Now extend your arms out to the sides, palms open and forward at the level of the heart. Feel how energy moves out horizontally from the center of your heart, out through your arms and hands and into the world. Christian teaching shows us that by opening the heart, Christ consciousness can be realized and acted upon. It is through the heart that we put spirit in action.*

*Try to maintain the sense of both currents of energy passing through you, from the top of your head to the earth, and from the heart radiating out to the sides. You are now a living cross, an expression of commitment to love and service. Remain in this meditation for as long as is comfortable. No repetition is necessary. Become aware once again of your breathing. Amen.*

When I practice this meditation, I feel connected to a healing source of sacred dance. Several years ago I had the good fortune of being introduced to the Sacred Dance Guild, an organization that was founded in 1958 to explore and re-create dance as a sacred expression in the worship services in Christian churches of all denominations and in Jewish synagogues. The guild is a nonprofit, interdenominational organization open to all who share a common interest in dance as a language of worship and celebration. The majority of its six hundred members work within their local churches and synagogues, but the guild also sponsors public events and festivals at which various dance forms from different religious, cultural, and ethnic backgrounds are performed. Members and guests are given the opportunity to experience movement as worship, prayer, healing, and meditation. (Information for contacting the Sacred Dance Guild is given in the back of this book.)

## UNIVERSALITY OF SACRED MOVEMENT AND GESTURE

Throughout time and across many cultures, sacred dance has played a vital role in society, connecting, revitalizing, and guiding us to our inner spiritual center. As you begin to experiment with the gestures and dances throughout this book, you may find that they feel vaguely familiar to you. The language of dance is universal to all humans. To explain dance's common appeal, Martha Graham had a theory of "blood memory," which referred to the inheritance of ancestral movements and gestures.

Graham believed in the physical memory of the body. I, too, believe that you can tap into this memory through embodied prayer. In almost every culture of the world, a gesture of reaching up toward the sky acts as an invocation, while prayers for the gifts of life are often directed toward the earth. Gestures for emotional and physical pain may contract the body into a semifetal position. Rocking motions symbolize and offer comfort, while leaping expresses joy, openness, and power.

This common language of movement is often unconsciously translated into our everyday lives. Sacred dance movements can connect you with the present. If raising your hand is an invocation of a call to attention, then perhaps you can notice the language of dance when you hail a cab or reach for your groceries when you shop. Reaching down to pull on your shoes can be a reminder to stay connected to the earth and walk with healing intention throughout your day. Reaching for a glass in an upper cupboard can be a reminder to reach for your highest dream. Perhaps you can think of other possibilities.

When you become more aware of your movements, you can make a conscious decision to move purposefully, with grace and beauty. Your affirmation of mindful movements will enable you to see life as a sacred dance—one of great beauty, power, and complexity.

The history of sacred dance continues today through the bodies and souls of you and me as we learn how to move our own spirits into action. The poet Theodore Roethke wrote, "I learn by going where I have to go." Take the first step. Join the circle and make it whole.

## Chapter 3

# THE BODY AS SACRED SPACE

*The body is composed of different organs and millions of cells. Each cell is a shell containing a soul spark. Therefore, the body is a physical shell for millions of soul sparks.*

—RABBI DAVID A. COOPER, *GOD IS A VERB*

## THE DIVINE AUTHOR OF THE BODY

The body is a miracle. Genesis 1:31 says, "God saw every thing that It had made, and, behold, it was very good. . . ." Our bodies and souls together express the wonders of Creation. Attitudes holding that the body lacks inherent goodness run contrary to God's own intention. When we accept ourselves as part of this wonder, we understand that our humanity is a gift from the Divine.

Celeste Snowber Schroeder, in her book *Embodied Prayer*, writes, "Christianity is an incarnational faith. The very fact of the incarnation affirms the body as part of God's intentional design. We are our bodies, and if God can honor the body enough to be revealed through flesh, we need to take the body seriously." The devaluation of the body by some interpreters and preachers of Western religions may be why so many people feel fragmented emotionally and psychologically and turn to drugs, food, alcohol, and a host of other addictive behaviors to feed some senses and avoid feeling others. We are made to feel self-conscious at any spontaneous expression of joy or enthusiasm outside of the limited routines that society mandates.

Women typically have a difficult time trusting that our bodies are sacred space due to a long history of misogynist attitudes toward women in general and toward women's bodies specifically, especially on the part of the Church fathers. Celeste Snowber Schroeder emphasizes this in *Embodied Prayer* and cites numerous examples. For instance, Tertullian in the second century called women "the devil's gateway." A century later Origen taught that man is more closely associated with God because woman is fleshly and opposite to anything divine. Augustine in the fourth century denied that women are made in God's image, and Aquinas in the thirteenth century declared that women are "misbegotten males," formed from "some unsuitability of material."

For many centuries women's bodies have been blamed for male carnal desire, and women along with their bodies have been denigrated as inferior to men. On a conscious level most intelligent people of both sexes are repelled at these attitudes today, but they have been instilled into our theology, culture, and philosophy on an unconscious level. They still persist at least subliminally and often overtly in movies, advertising, TV shows, office politics, sports, and religious organizations.

Men, too, have been affected by attitudes that bodily pleasure is not spiritual or is even outright sinful in nature. Both men and women have been affected by the wounding of the mind and soul caused by negative attitudes toward the physical body. When guilt drives culture, it deprives us of the vision of a creative, nurturing, passionate Divinity, a Creator who moves in the realms of unconditional love, inner knowing, and intuitive wisdom. The model of spirituality for which many people deeply yearn is that of the ever-compassionate Holy Companion, who whispers love and acceptance to us under the din of worldly noise.

Through the beauty of nature, however, we know that our capacity to use our five senses must come from the Creator. We can find joy in all these senses, and all of it feeds our hearts—the physical and metaphorical seat of love, compassion, and connection. When we use our body to express the breath of the Great Spirit, we are living fully in ourselves and on the earth.

# FACING OUR LIMITATIONS
## WITH COMPASSION

When we first include our bodies in prayerful and meditative movement, we learn lessons about their strengths as well as their weaknesses. When you acknowledge your physical limitations—limitations of endurance, flexibility, or gracefulness—accept your body's abilities with compassion. This will lead you to your own personal starting point.

You need not be an experienced dancer to put spirit in action. If you have never taken a dance class, that's just fine. Your body, too, is just fine. Start where you are. Do not have unreasonable expectations; you want to enjoy yourself in this new practice. Many people who have attended my workshops have overcome any initial sense of awkwardness by approaching these movements with a sense of play.

One of my students, Zoie, is a ninety-five-year-old woman who dances despite the physical limitations of her age. When I asked her if it took courage to attend a dance class like mine, her eyes lit up, and she said:

> This prayerful dance gives me vitality and energy. It helps me to move forward in my life, instead of regretting the life I've left unlived or all the things I can no longer do. I do what I can and move at peace with my body. It's a new idea; it brings me new life; it keeps me looking forward. I want to dance into the arms of God at my passing.

This enlightened view of aging helps us to accept our physical limitations while remaining unafraid of dying. Rabbi Zalman Schachter Shalomi, author of *Aging into Saging* and the audiotape *Spiritual Eldering*, says that most people approach old age and death as if they were walking backward into a room. They don't want to acknowledge the inevitable, feeling that it's "better not to look at it." His message encourages us to embrace the wisdom of our years and life experiences, the fullness and "the harvest" that aging provides. It's the same message that Zoie was able to experience for herself through prayerful movement.

No matter our limitations, when we begin to practice embodied prayer, Spirit watches over us with love and enjoyment, welcoming our attempts at connection. If we listen carefully, we can hear the sound of warm cosmic laughter and applause.

# WOMEN'S BODIES AS SOURCES OF CREATIVITY

Many women intuitively understand the divine model of an unconditionally compassionate Creator because the rhythms and cycles of creation are reflected in our bodies. This is wisdom that we understand deep within us, in every cell of our bodies, with a physical knowing that bypasses the mind. Women are further programmed by our genes and our culture to give unconditional love to the children we birth. Whether or not a woman chooses to conceive and birth children, the awareness of this creative capacity is hardwired into our psyches as well as into our bodies. We can learn to bring compassion and innate bodily wisdom to all of our creative ability, whether that be writing, dancing, managing a stock portfolio, solving relationship challenges, or raising children. The body is a holy site, a sacred temple of the Creative Source, and sacred dance and embodied prayer are effective means of connecting us to this inner wisdom.

I recently received a letter from Janine, a woman in her late thirties who had taken a sacred dance workshop with me in Seattle a few years ago. The experience she related echoes the voices and comments of many women to whom I've introduced embodied prayer. One evening, during a stay at the Tassajara retreat center in central California, she had taken a leisurely soak in a hot tub, then found herself drawn to a small creek with low-lying mists. The moon was full, and in the beauty of the night, she began to move spontaneously through a pattern of embodied prayers I had taught her. After a few repetitions, she began to make up her own dances, which seemed to be coming to her from her cellular memory of a connection to an ancient origin and power. That evening the dances opened up a creative space in her soul that she was able to bring back into her everyday life and heal herself from a long empty spell. She had been stuck and unable to move forward, yet after the evening of dancing her own embodied prayers, something had shifted within her. She became able to ask creative questions about her own life: Does my life reflect who I am now? What are my options? How can I create what I want by utilizing the unique perspective and process of my womanly wisdom?

The sense of "remembered sacred dancing" is common to the women in my workshops, no matter their age, background, or ethnicity. Perhaps this is what Martha Graham also meant by her term *blood memory*. Knowledge of dance, the body as prayer, flows in our blood. Sometimes I feel as if I do not need to teach the path of sacred dance to women but simply say, "Wake up! Remember!"

# HEALING THE MALE/FEMALE SPLIT IN OUR CULTURE

Although women have more generally and more frequently connected, and realized when they need to reconnect, the body to their experience of the sacred, a growing number of men are also trying to bring the body into their personal experience of worship. Men and women participating together in sacred dance and embodied prayer help heal themselves and one another and bridge the cultural rift and distrust between the sexes that patriarchal religions and philosophies have fostered for centuries. Men and women move differently, and the strength and grounded qualities of men, together with the lighter, sometimes quicker movements of women, inspire a vision of divine balance working in the Universe. We each are expressions of the male and female faces of God; we each possess male and female energies. Our energies working in concert with one another express the physics of the Life force itself and reflect the ancient concept of the yin (female, earthy, passive, receptive, represented by water and the moon) balanced by the yang (male, heavenly, active, penetrating, represented by fire and the sun), both energies arising from the Ultimate Oneness.

Unfortunately, in our Western culture, men who are willing to explore their physical expression in sacred dance activities are exposing themselves to ridicule. In other cultures, however, men do most of the dancing and are at home in their bodies as vehicles of expressive worship. Native American men swirl in bustles and headdresses; Aborigine men dance in a corroboree; dervish mystics twirl. These men enthusiastically bring the fullness of their experience into their strong, exuberant dances.

# SACRED SEXUALITY

Let my beloved come into his garden,
let him taste its rarest fruits.
—*THE SONG OF SONGS*

Freeing the body so that it can be an integral part of our spirituality also helps us become more conscious of the energy of sexuality. Sexuality is not limited to the act of sex. It is one part of our being that influences how we see the world and how we act in the world, how we connect to others, and how we express our spirituality. Our sexuality calls forth the deep yearning for union, at the core of which is the desire for union with our Divine Source—a yearning to be made whole in body, mind, and spirit.

This yearning is made manifest in the passionate union with a lover. By seeing our lover as part of a sacred calling, we change the context of our sexual expression. It becomes more than physical, a holy realm. This is a time-honored perspective, perhaps most famously explored by the Persian mystic Jalal ad-Din ar-Rumi, whom we know today as the poet Rumi. In many of his poems, he directs his narrative to his "Beloved," including within that name that part of Divinity that is immanent in all things.

FROM *THE ILLUMINATED RUMI*

My place is
The placeless, a trace
Of the traceless.
Neither body or soul.

I belong to the Beloved,
Have seen the two
Worlds as one and
That one
Call to and know.

First, last, outer, inner.
Only that breath breathing
Human being.

Sacred holy rituals were integrated into the practice of sexuality in cultures such as Indian Tantric yoga, the old religion of the Celts, and some Native American traditions. Tantric yoga temples in India were once holy places where the women priestesses, called Tantricas, taught the arts of sensuality and sexuality as a vehicle to open the heart consciousness of the male initiates who came there. Sexuality was viewed as more than genital—a complete mind-body-spirit practice. At their highest development these sexual practices were considered an enlightened yogic path. When British colonialists found remnants of these temples with sexually explicit sculptures mimicking the sexual postures of the Kama Sutra, they considered them lewd vestiges of a wanton civilization rather than evidence of the sacred potential of sexuality as a holy rite.

In Celtic, pre-Christian Europe, May 1 was the holy day of Beltane, or May Day. Sexuality celebrated outdoors in open, plowed fields was an integral part of the rites performed on this holy day. The women were seen as embodying the fertile fields of the Earth Mother herself, the Great Goddess personified. The men acted as holy consorts, fertilizing women in the fields as a way to ensure fruitful crops for the growing season. Children born of a Beltane union were considered a special blessing to the community.

## ∼ Lakota Sex Ritual ∼

*Another example of sacred sexuality is seen in the Lakota nation. The following is a sacred Lakota ritual that I learned from Lori Grace, a California teacher of world Tantra. To perform this sacred, embodied ritual, you will need three glasses, one of which must be fireproof, such as a Pyrex, Corningware, or a fired ceramic container. You will also need a piece of paper and a pen or pencil, some ground cornmeal, candles, and sacred, personal objects, such as photos, wedding bands, journals, or other talismans of your choice.*

*To prepare for the ritual, fill one glass halfway with white wine and the other with the same amount of red wine. White and red grape juice may be substituted. The fireproof glass or container remains empty. Next, as a couple, you need to agree upon a clear, prayerful intention—such as healing a family member, healing the earth, or bringing a new soul to birth—which you will write on the piece of paper.*

*The ritual begins with an act of purification, whether it be a bath, smudging with the smoke of burning sage, or massaging each other. During the purification, each person should clear his or her mind of extraneous thoughts and focus on the present moment.*

*Once you have completed the act of purification, create a sacred circle in whatever way you feel is appropriate. You may create a circle on the earth or floor with ground cornmeal, lit candles, or the sacred, personal objects listed earlier. The circle affirms that you have created holy ground and should enter it with reverence.*

*With both partners in the circle, the woman prays aloud to invoke the presence of the Earth Mother, the grandmother spirits, her ancestors, and spirit guides to bear witness and bless her part in the rite. Her partner listens attentively. When she has completed her prayer, the man invites Father Sky, the grandfather spirits, his ancestors, and spirit guides similarly. When he has completed his prayers, they read aloud the prayer they wrote down earlier.*

*After sanctifying your interaction with prayer, you begin to make love within the circle. During your lovemaking, hold this prayerful intention in mind, using the energy of your passion to intensify and honor your mutual purpose.*

*When your lovemaking is concluded, the woman drinks part of the red wine, which symbolizes the blood of her creative powers. The man drinks part of the white wine, which symbolizes the semen of his creative powers. Together, you place your written affirmation in the fireproof glass or container. In a safe place, perhaps outside, set the paper on fire and, as the smoke rises to the sky, ask that the Great Spirit accept your prayer. When there is nothing left in the container but ashes, the woman pours the remaining red wine into the glass, and the man does the same with the white wine, to symbolize the mixing of their energies in creative, prayerful purpose.*

*To complete the ritual, the couple takes the glass to a tree, bush, or houseplant and waters the earth with the symbolic purpose of bringing their intention to fruition.*

This entire ritual, from preparation to conclusion, helps us to see the body and natural acts of pleasure as a gift from the Great Spirit to be celebrated and offered back as an act of prayer and healing.

## MOVEMENT FOR HEALING THE MIND AND BODY

Including the body in your spiritual expression brings healing on many levels, physical and emotional. Although I conceived *The Aerobic Prayer Series* as a means to deepen spiritual life and reinforce the concept of the body as a vehicle for prayer, I was awed and surprised by the healing tears that many women experienced as their body and spirit flowed together.

Embodied prayers seem to have a healing effect on many women who suffer from clinical depression. This kind of depression is due to an imbalance of neurotransmitters in the brain. When in balance, these "emotional chemicals" allow us to feel safe, content, and confident. Clinical depression is different from situational depression, which develops in response to an event such as divorce or the death of a child, although situational depression can develop into clinical depression. The active ingredient in many commonly prescribed anti-depressants such as Prozac, Zoloft, and the herbal compound Saint-John's-wort works by stabilizing the amount of the neurotransmitter serotonin in the brain, which allows us to feel calmer, more content, and accepting. Researchers in sports medicine have proved that aerobic activity helps to combat low-level depression by stabilizing serotonin and by releasing another set of neurotransmitters called endorphins, which have been shown to help overcome physical and emotional pain.

One of my students, Eve, came to my classes in a devastated emotional state. For more than fifteen years, Eve had suffered from a depression that caused her to isolate herself in her home, watch endless hours of television while splayed on her couch, and simply not leave. Her depression had become her life.

A friend of hers dragged her to her first dance class with me, and Eve actually left after the session with a sparkle in her eye that surprised us all. After a few weeks she told me, "The dancing prayers are great. I feel alive for the first time in years." Eve wasn't suddenly free from her demons, but her commitment to physical activity helped her find the energy and hope to engage in other pursuits in her life.

I also believe that the spirituality inherent in the dances provided a framework for Eve to connect to something that was outside of her small, isolated world. She was able to see beyond herself, make a soul connection, and from there strive to bring vitality into her entire life. When I see Eve today, I barely recognize the woman who first came to take a class with me.

Sacred dance can call us out of habitual, negative patterns. Embodied prayer provides us with energy and a sense of inner well-being and health. It helps to connect us to our bodies by making us feel that we are an integral part of the circle of life.


To heal any physical trauma or violation of part of our being, it is imperative to include the body in the process. With all the mixed messages our culture conveys regarding our bodies and sensuality, many people feel alienated from their physical nature. Sacred dance frees both physical and emotional energy that can help catalyze inner healing.

One woman described her experience this way:

For many years I had experienced a sense of heaviness in my abdomen and hips. This is also where I carry extra weight. I had never really connected this with the sexual abuse of my youth. When I started to use *The Aerobic Prayer Series* to move my body with prayerful intention, it was as if a huge stagnant mass of blocked energy in my pelvis dissolved. I was able to mobilize and dissipate the victimized part of myself. I found myself crying tears of release and joy. My body was telling me that everything was okay. The programs gave me permission to bring my body along on my spiritual journey.

Spirit creates our bodies and infuses them with the Life Force. When we move in prayerful intention, that energy surfaces from the depth of our bones, from the deepest corners of our being. We become our prayer energy in motion. Frozen emotions and traumas are forced to the surface and exposed to the healing light of Spirit, creating more room in our bodies for healthy energy, flexibility, and joy. This is the healing wisdom of the body.

A few years ago I had the privilege of facilitating a workshop that was attended by a woman in her mid-forties who had been left partially paralyzed by a brain aneurysm several years before. She had suffered through years of agonizingly slow progress as she learned how to walk again and perform the simplest of daily tasks. When she came to me, she was looking for a way to include her body in a spiritual practice. We adapted the embodied prayers so that she performed most of them with her upper body only. I was in awe of the intensity of her focus and commitment and was delighted that prayerful movement had such a positive effect on her.

Over time she told me that she was able to "get her rhythm back," thanks to the combination of music and the dances. She was able to find her rhythm and call on that energy during her physical therapy sessions. Slowly her gait improved, and she now often walks without the support of her cane. She is able to translate the benefits of Aerobic Prayer into the activities of her daily movements. She exudes a very powerful sense of "being in her body" and accepting her limitations that is inspirational.

## ⌒ Miracle of the Body Meditation ⌒

*Ask someone you trust to read the following meditation to you slowly, then read it to him or her, or tape-record the meditation.*

*Begin in any comfortable position, sitting or lying. Breathe quietly and deeply, letting each breath fill your abdomen. Feel your body relaxing from your midsection out through your extremities as each breath flows through you and from you. Notice your feet. Loosely move your toes, exploring the complexity of their movement. Now move each part of your feet and ankles. Contract them. Expand them. Rotate them. Give thanks for the work of your beautiful feet. Consider how they connect you to the earth. Bless your feet that they may continue to carry you on the spiritual path. Breathe quietly and deeply.*

*Move your attention and awareness into your legs and give thanks for the strength they exhibit as they hold you up and root you to the earth. Now sense the warm wave of relaxation coming up through the feet into the legs and let the muscles of your calves relax and the muscles of your thighs relax. Breathe quietly and deeply.*

*Notice your hips and pelvis. Move any way you wish to loosen the hips and let the wave of relaxation flow into your hips and spread through your pelvis. Give thanks for the pelvic bowl, which carries the source of your creativity. With each breath feel the creative force flowing in and feel gratitude extending out into the Universe as you let each breath out.*

*Allow your lower back to receive this blessing as well and feel the relaxation spread up your spine and around into your abdomen. Thank your spine for the work it does as the support for your body. Breathe deeply and quietly.*

*Bring your awareness into the chest and upper back. Allow your chest to melt into the wave of relaxation and, as you loosen the chest, notice the region of your heart opening more and more. Give thanks for your sacred heart and allow its capacity to receive and offer love expand to fill the Universe.*

*Release a wave of relaxation and let it flow through the shoulders and down the arms all the way to your hands. Give thanks for all the expressions of love that your arms and hands provide. Bless them for their service. Breathe quietly and deeply.*

*Feel the relaxation move up into your neck, jaw, mouth, and tongue. Allow this feeling to deepen as your mind forms the intention, "May my mouth speak only what is true in my heart."*

*Let your eyes relax and become very heavy. Let your forehead soften. Let your eyes provide you with clear vision and allow only clear guidance to flow into your mind.*

*Be aware that your body resides in safety within your spirit. Notice how comfortable and peaceful you are. Enjoy this state as long as you wish. Be blessed. When you are ready, open your eyes and take this peace and blessedness within you out into the world.*

# Chapter 4

# MOVEMENT AS MANTRA

*Ecstasy is an ideal, a goal, but it can be the expectation of everyday life. Those times when we are grounded in our body, pure in our heart, clear in our mind, rooted in our soul, and suffused with the energy, the spirit of life, are our birthright.*

—GABRIELLE ROTH, *MAPS TO ECSTASY*

A mantra is a word, sound, or phrase that is repeated to calm and focus the mind. The practice of mantra is thought to have originated in India. However, its influence is evident in the ancient languages of Hebrew and Aramaic in the Middle East many centuries before the birth of Christ. Many of these ancient languages shared a common understanding that the repetition of certain sounds—and of course, movements—could cause powerful vibrational changes in consciousness. The essence of mantra is that through certain sounds we can experience the Oneness (God) interpenetrating form (the body). We are able to commune with the Divine manifesting on all three levels—body, mind, and spirit.

# FOCUS OF ATTENTION

The sound of a mantra acts as a focus of attention for the linear part of the brain. Keeping the brain occupied with the sound encourages the mind to let go of the ordinary noise of cerebral activity that chatters away all day. After we quiet our distracting thoughts, our attention is free to go beyond surface concerns and into deeper states of awareness. Mantra is a valuable aid for helping us hear the still, small voice within.

A mantra may or may not have a literal meaning. A friend of mind found the word *selah* in the psalms and was intrigued because some sources said it had no defined meaning, whereas others claimed it was a musical direction, since the psalms were originally meant to be sung. *Selah,* a word he stumbled on, has become his personal mantra, and he uses it to enter a meditative state or recalls it when life is hectic and he needs to cut to the chase of his own true thoughts.

You, too, may choose to create your own mantra with a term like *love* or *peace* or *Divine Light* or *Beloved Friend* or *om*, the ancient sound indicating oneness. You can increase the power of a mantra with a gesture in which you have invested a spiritual significance. Whatever word or phrase you choose carries with it a particular emotional and vibrational quality that personalizes your meditation. Only when the active mind quiets can we listen to the deep, intuitive wisdom within us.

Repetition is the key to success. Regular meditation is a discipline that works over time, so that even when you are not actively meditating, your thought patterns become calmer and more organized. Repetition of the mantra prepares the mind, but the act of meditation itself must also be repeated frequently. This carryover into everyday life is the goal at the heart of every spiritual discipline, from meditation to prayer.

Because our brains seem to have a mind of their own and thoughts arise from unknown origins, it sometimes takes a while to see the effects of our inner practice translate into benefits such as calmness, equanimity, and greater perspective in our outer lives. Scientific studies support the idea that much repetition is necessary to create new neurological pathways of thought and reroute habitual emotional responses. We have to change the neurochemistry of our brain physically, by mental and emotional activity. This is not accomplished by having one good thought but by having a determined multitude.

The first astronauts believed that wars would instantly cease when the first photographs of the Earth from space were made available around the world, for we would all see ourselves as connected and united on one planet. Although one image could not instantly retrain the brain chemistry that creates fear and confrontation, we can decide individually to change our thinking, expand our range of emotional responses to work on our own inner peace—which will help create peace in the world around us.

## MOVING MANTRAS

Like the repetition of sound, the repetition of movement can have a powerful influence on the body and mind. Eventually, you integrate the physical pattern into your nervous and musculoskeletal systems, and it becomes automatic. Repetitive movements can help you become proficient at connecting your mind with your body and with your spiritual energy. Movements and postures—or moving mantras, as I like to call them—can quiet the mind and help focus it into a deep awareness. Like chanted mantras, moving mantras can have specific meanings, or they can just be an effective motion that focuses your attention.

Most of the moving mantras in this book do carry specific meanings and are linked to prayerful intentions. For instance, if the verbal prayer or song that I've suggested to go with the physical movement talks about opening the heart, I've created movements and gestures that open the arms widely to the sides to expand the chest and heart area. If the lyrics or prayers speak of sending a bless-

*Opening the heart*

*Sending a blessing*

ing to the world, the gesture may send the hand out in an attitude of blessing. Following the movements of your hands with your eyes adds intention and focus to the act and sends the energy out around you.

I find that the effects of performing moving meditations follow me throughout my day. For instance, if a moving prayer combines a reach for higher guidance and wisdom that reverses into a low, grounded, packing movement, that sequence can symbolize a "seeding" of wisdom into the earth. Later, as I work in my garden, that gesture reminds me of my commitment to sprout actions that reflect wisdom and compassion in my everyday life. I will also feel this "parallel physicality" at my job, as I make decisions that affect me, my loved ones, and even strangers. This carryover into the rest of life is the magic of a moving mantra. By repeatedly engaging the body in moving prayers, we tune our minds to live each moment of every day in sync with spiritual energy. When we bring our bodies fully into praying with movement, we are saying, "I will create my spiritual goals in the physical world. I will be fully engaged, fully embodied emotionally, physically, and spiritually." This is a powerful affirmation for creating heaven on earth!

In moving mantras we use the wisdom of the body-mind to call the breath of the Great Spirit into our physical world. These embodied prayers help focus our intentions, actualize our goals, and bring forth the deep wisdom in our bones. We say our prayer with every part of our being.

To illustrate the power of a moving mantra, I have adapted the following exercise from Rabbi David Cooper's book *Entering the Sacred Mountain*. Rabbi Cooper uses the mantra "Devekut" (pronounced Deh-veh-KOOT), which means "to cling or to melt into God." In his book he writes, "Jewish mystics believe this letting go of the boundaries of the self is a high state of illumination—giving up one's will in a union of pure love where there is no clear distinction between lover and beloved."

### ∿ Melting into the Beloved ∿

*To perform this moving mantra, begin in a seated position and close your eyes. Sit up straight, with your feet on the floor. Rock your torso to the front and back, placing your right hand in front of your left shoulder and your left hand in front of your right shoulder. Repeat one syllable of the mantra on each forward and each backward movement of the torso. Feel the sense of letting go and melting into the Beloved One. Stay with this meditation for as long as you like. I like to do this for fifteen to twenty minutes, but you may want to start with no more than five minutes. When you are finished, sit in stillness for a minute or two and feel the energy this moving mantra has created within you. Gradually open your eyes. Inhale and exhale slowly and deeply three times and complete the meditation by affirming that you will take this sense of peaceful surrender into the rest of your life.*

# THE USES OF MOVING MANTRA

## CONGRUITY

Congruity is agreement between a person's words, body language, and verbal expressiveness. Experts in the fields of linguistics and neurolinguistic programming agree that body language is the most important aspect of communication, accounting for approximately 55 percent of the meaning expressed. Verbal expression contributes about 38 percent of our meaning, and the actual words we use account for only about 7 percent. When the meanings of these three aspects of our communications don't match, we are incongruent or out of sync with ourselves and other people. To take the pulse of your own congruency, try this:

> Thrust your shoulders forward in an exaggerated slump. Now slump your spinal posture as well and hang your head forward and down. Put a frown on your face. Now say, "Boy, am I in a good mood!" and try to feel joyous and optimistic. It doesn't work, does it? There's no body energy driving the emotion. There's no life to the words.

Now put your body into the opposite mode:

> Stand up tall. Lift your chest up and thrust your shoulders back. Hold your head up high. Smile broadly and confidently. Stride confidently around the room. Now continue to smile and say, "Boy, am I depressed!" That doesn't work either, does it? Anyone watching you won't buy your words.

Okay, now really go for it. Head high, broad smile. Say, "I'm in a great mood!" How does that feel, now that you're being congruent?

When movement is united with prayerful intentions, we create congruity within the mind-body.

## THE "AS IF" FRAME

Congruity also applies to our deeper affirmations and our prayers. Affirmation is the act of telling ourselves and others that a thing or situation exists. It might be something as simple and concrete as "The sky is blue." It might be as abstract as, "People are inherently good-hearted, and everyone I meet treats me with compassion and understanding." When we put the energy of our bodies into agreement with the thought behind an affirmation, our minds accept the affirmation as the truth. In other words, we create congruity between our actions and attitudes. Our minds then create an energy that leads to the realization of that which we are affirming.

Bringing our bodies into the process of affirmation enhances the realization of our life goals. This is a classic "as if" frame. We define that which we desire by creating a "frame" around it in our minds and acting as if it were already true. When we act as if we already have what we really want, or we act as if we already are that which we wish to be, we tend to mold reality from congruity of our feelings and beliefs. Salespeople use the "as if" frame when they try to sell you something by using what's called the "assumptive close." You may still be deciding whether you want what they're selling or not, and they ask, "Do you want that in green or blue?" They skip the question "Do you want it at all?" They consciously assume that you want it and act as if you'd already agreed to buy it. The more congruent the salesperson becomes—the more he acts as if you've already agreed to buy the thing and truly believes in his own mind that you want the item—the more likely you are to respond, "I'll take it in blue."

This may sound a bit incredible, but neuroscientific studies support this idea. Our brain cells connect in certain patterns, some of which are determined by DNA and early life experiences. The brain will use an established pathway when processing information, just as you drive the same road to and from your house and to and from your office, day after day. But what if one day there were a roadblock and you had to choose a new route? You'd have to find a different route, just as the brain has to form new pathways when it must respond to something new. When we use our imagination to visualize a frequent problem and then visualize a different outcome or script, the brain cells actually realign themselves. The part of the brain that is responsible for changes of this sort is called the "anterior attentional network." The stronger the new mental picture we present to the brain, the more likely the brain cells are to realign themselves in response to it. The more congruent we are—the more we align our physical energy and mental attitude to conform to the new image we are creating—the stronger the new mental picture will be. A free-ranging imagination, intention, and congruity are the key elements in creating meaningful life changes.

To illustrate the principle of realigning body and brain for congruity in my workshops, I use martial arts movements. The various kicks and strikes are wonderful expressions of explosive power and assertion. These moves become physical metaphors for banishing something undesirable from your life and for drawing something you truly desire into your life. The following is a wonderful exercise for building a strong sense of willpower.

## ∽ Moving Mantra—Connecting to Your Goal ∽

*Begin standing with your feet shoulder-width apart, arms hanging comfortably at your sides. Close your eyes and hold the image of a goal toward which you really want to work. Then open your eyes and choose a spot on the floor, wall, or ceiling and let that spot represent your goal. If you are a beginner, choose a spot on the floor as your goal. If you are more advanced, you can place your image up on the wall within your kicking comfort zone. You will be kicking through your heel toward that spot. This means that your foot remains flexed during the kick so that the energy of the kick comes down the leg and right out through the sole of your foot. Be careful not to snap or hyperextend your knee when you kick. Take a moment to inhale and exhale three times deeply, sending energy through your body and down into your legs, the focus point of movement in this exercise.*

*The movement begins with what's called a grapevine step in four counts. Step to the right side with your right foot and continue to move to the right by bringing the left foot directly behind the right. Step your right foot to the right again. Then, with your weight balanced on your right foot, bring your left leg to the point of your goal and kick through your heel toward that spot. Bull's-eye! Reverse to the left side and repeat the movement, this time kicking with your right foot.*

*I like to repeat the movement twenty to fifty times. Of course, this depends on your physical ability. Honor your body's comfort zone. It's crucial to maintain your sense of focus, intention, and follow-through. You are mentally willing your body to connect with your intended goal. You're tapping into conscious and unconscious power.*

A woman who used to be in my classes in northern California, Beth, seemed as if she had it all together. Bright, sensitive, attractive, and successful, Beth actually had a manipulative streak and a very circuitous manner of getting what she wanted. Her communication style was often incongruous with her message. She waffled in her plans and in speaking her own mind, so her life was a series of "almosts." Her business wasn't doing as well as it could have been; she was profoundly ambivalent about her companion; she vacillated between living in the city or the country. She had a low-grade misery.

Over the course of several months in my classes, Beth progressed in her practice of the kicking exercise. Initially she had a very difficult time understanding and accepting its power, and her kicks were wishy-washy, directed vaguely into space instead of directly toward the spot representing her goal. Her steps clearly reflected her interior life. Over two or three months, she began to move—and speak—with directness. If she didn't understand a direction, she would let me know. She would hold her space in class if another dancer tried to cut ahead of her. The transformation was amazing, and it carried over into other parts of her life. Beth shared with me that one of her goals was to write and publish a book she had been thinking about for years. She decided to cut back her office hours and found that she was able to maintain and even surpass her income in fewer hours per week. Her book was soon well under way. She also realized that her boyfriend was a "maybe" and that "maybe" is not "yes." She moved on and discovered that she loved living alone, being fully in charge of her life.

When our minds and bodies work together to become clear and congruent, we can channel our energy to make almost miraculous changes in our lives.

## DEVELOPING PHYSICAL IMAGINATION

Moving mantras have a transformative power. Because you are expressing your imagination physically, acting as if you already possessed the qualities you desire, you build new, strong patterns into your neurology and body. Your body becomes congruent with your mind, and both become in sync with your spirit. Achieving congruity of body, mind, and spirit is one of the steps toward spiritual maturity, which is the larger goal of our lives.

Spiritual maturity means meeting life's challenges with appropriate behavior and a peaceful, centered attitude. Here is an exploration that will help you learn how to attain emotional balance. This moving mantra initially has a narrow, defined, pointed intention and then switches to a softer, more open focus. Although the physical step remains the same, as you change your intention, the feeling of the movement and meditation changes. If you have trouble becoming centered, the initial focused part of the dance will probably be more challenging. If you tend to focus intensely to the exclusion of freedom and joy, the part of the dance that uses soft focus and circular movements to express joyful abandon will probably feel foreign. As you practice both forms and switch back and forth, your brain learns the flexibility to expand its array of natural responses. You gather new internal resources by using the body as the vehicle of imaginative creation.

### ～ Moving Mantra—Balance between Focus and Joy ～

*Before you begin the actual movements in this exercise, put on some music with a definable beat. My preference for this exercise is music with Latin rhythms, but soft jazz can also work just fine. Begin standing with feet hip-width apart, knees slightly bent, and your arms hanging comfortably at your sides. Take several deep breaths and relax into the present moment. Then consider where in your life you need to use a tightly focused intention. Is it at work or at home? For me the feeling of tight focus expresses itself as a very linear, mechanical movement style. Carry that feeling of tight focus into the next movement.*

*First the footwork: Begin by raising up your right knee, then let it come back to starting position. Then step your left foot back, then return it to starting position. Repeat this eight to ten times, then switch sides, raising the left knee. Now the upper body: Let your hands be rigid. Bend your elbows and let your arms swing like a toy soldier. As your right knee comes up, your left hand comes up to shoulder height. As your right knee comes down, the left hand comes up. When you step back with your left foot, your right hand rises again. Bring the left foot back to the starting position while raising the right hand. Reverse this hand pattern when you switch the lead knee. Remember to keep the lines of all movement straight and mechanical. Do this for fifteen to thirty repetitions.*

*Now change your focus from mechanical repetition of the step to an image of fluid movement. Continue with the same step but see whether you can "dance it." Let loose. Purposely move in more circuitous patterns. Let your hands and torso move freely. Let go of tight focus and lighten up. Are there places in your life where you could choose the joyful dance more often? Continue this for the same number of repetitions as you performed the first step. Now switch back to the focused step again, this time leading with the opposite knee up. How did the transition feel? Continue to switch back and*

forth between linear and circular movement for five to six transitions. End this movement by standing in stillness for a few moments and appreciate your ability to stand in balance.

Which of these patterns feels more natural to you? Most of us *find that we habitually hang out on one side of this spectrum more than the other. Playing with the pattern can help you balance your state of mind. As you shift back and forth consciously in the physical movement, you rewire your brain to become more adept at consciously choosing your inner state of attention.*

You can actually alter your mood by movement. If you are feeling stuck and rigid in your life, you can move consciously to lighten up: your brain gets the message from your body and goes along with the physical cue. Changing your movement can help you change your attitude.

Let's try something else. The following is an exercise from the grandmother of sacred dance in the United States, Ruth St. Denis, a pioneer in the world of movement as a spiritual practice. She was instrumental in reviving classical Indian dance in India, where it had become degraded as an art form. Her work influenced many of the leaders in the modern dance world of her time, including her former student Martha Graham.

In *Wisdom Comes Dancing*, author Kamae Miller writes that St. Denis gave this exercise to a Christian audience, although you are invited to substitute the appropriate figure from your own spiritual tradition or practice for Jesus, whether that be Buddha, Kuan-Yin, Mother Mary, Moses, or the Holy Prophet. St. Denis wrote:

What would we do if we were manifesting the Christ? Would not the rhythm of our walk, the posture of our bodies, the gestures that we make in work and play be of a different order? And the thoughts that motivate our movements—would they not be from a higher source?

## ∼ Walking in Spiritual Dominion ∼

*Walk around the room for the next several minutes as you think you would walk if you were to walk in spiritual dominion or maturity. Notice the rhythm that seems natural. Does your facial expression change? Your posture? How are you breathing? Create a sense of union with all beings. Spiritual dominion implies a natural stewardship. How do you manifest this stewardship? How can you bring this sense of caring and compassion into your own life? Continue to walk in dominion and allow yourself to receive messages from your body. The wisdom of your body can be your spiri-*

*tual teacher. Know that you can return to this state whenever you want to tap into the inner strength and wisdom of the great spiritual teachers to meet a challenge in your own life.*

## TRANSFORMING THE ENERGY OF NEGATIVE EMOTIONS

*"How will we know if he is truly a great teacher?" The Baal Shem Tov replied, "Ask him to advise you on what to do to keep unholy thoughts from disturbing your prayers and your studies." Then the master continued, "If this teacher gives you advice, you will know that he is not worthy. For it is the service of every person to struggle every hour until their death with extraneous thoughts and bring them into harmony with the nature of creation."*
—RABBI DAVID A. COOPER, *GOD IS A VERB*

We *can* learn to transform the energy behind a negative emotion—such as fear, anger, scattered thinking, or jealousy—to serve a higher purpose. Whenever we detect that one of these emotions is driving us, we can choose to transform it by first recognizing the negativity and then separating ourselves from it.

### Transforming Anger

For example, we can tell ourselves, "There is anger present," rather than, "I am angry." This separates out the emotion from us, from our internal state, or from the person to whom we're directing our anger. We refuse to identify with the anger. We acknowledge the negative energy in a general way, without accepting it as part of our personal makeup. This dissociation steps between the emotion and any action we might have taken to express it. We view the emotion as having simply attached itself to us, and now we have the opportunity to do something about it. We choose not to allow negativity to direct our lives.

The next step is to free our bodies from the effect of carrying negativity around inside us. The physical place in our bodies in which we tend to hold the energies of fear and anger is our solar plexus. Many of us may walk stiffly or slightly slumped as we try to carry these frozen, heavy emotions within us. We can use movement to thaw them. By imagining ourselves as joyful and free, and moving in ways that reflect these positive feelings, we release the negativity within us.

Try the following exercise.

## ∾ Releasing Anger ∾

*Begin standing in a relaxed position with your feet shoulder-width apart and your hands at your sides. Breathe slowly in and out three times. Think of something that has made you really angry. Acknowledge the presence of the anger by telling yourself, "Anger is present." Imagine angry energy clinging to your body like a grimy film of dust. Begin to walk around the room. Now tighten your fists as you walk. How does it feel to move wearing this cloak of negative energy? Do you notice any feelings of heaviness or constriction?*

*Now take a somewhat wide stance with your feet, bending your knees slightly. With your hands begin to vigorously brush this anger "dust" off you, exhaling sharply with each brush stroke. Imagine that you are sending the anger to the earth to be transformed. When you are finished, take three deep breaths, inhaling the spirit of healing and unity deeply into your body. Remember who you are. You are not your anger. Begin walking around the room again and consciously throw your shoulders back, raise your head up a few degrees, and allow a slight smile to brighten your face. Swing your arms freely. Remember a time when you were joyful and at peace in your world. Bring that memory to your body's gait. Continue to walk until you can fully transform the anger with which you started this exercise. End by standing in stillness, appreciating that you have the power to choose to release anger and move on.*

In this exercise we are acting as Spirit's recycling plant for negativity. We become alchemists, magicians of the practical. By focusing our mind on transformation while we put our body into motion, we use the energy of the unwanted emotion to create something new and useful in the world—for example, choosing harmony in our own relationships, which will extend peacefulness out into the world. From this perspective our emotional sensitivities give us the ability and dedication to clean up the energetic environment of the planet—a kind of spiritual ecology.

It's especially important to learn to express anger in healthy, appropriate ways, because it's an emotion that quickly becomes toxic to us if we don't have some way of transmuting it. Women often have difficulty allowing themselves to become angry because many have been taught that "ladies" don't get angry or don't express anger. As a result of not being true to what they feel, women suffer from depression, which is widely believed to be caused by unexpressed anger turned inward, more frequently than men. It is imperative that we all have an appropriate release for this naturally occurring human emotion so that we can get by it and move to healing. A variety of martial arts kicks and blocks are great for releasing this energy. I don't recommend that you use punching moves, because the elbow is a delicate joint, and it's very easy to injure by snapping a punch. I prefer to use the strength of the shoulder with an elbow block.

## ～ Expressing Anger and Moving On ～

*First, put on some loud music with a hard, driving beat. Begin standing with your feet planted a little wider than your shoulders and your knees bent slightly, about 15 to 20 degrees, depending on your level of comfort. Keep your abdominal muscles engaged slightly by partially tucking your pelvis under. This creates a stable position that will allow you to perform this exercise without engaging the lower back in any torque, which could be damaging. We'll begin the sequence of movement with elbow blocks. These are sharp backward thrusts of the elbow at shoulder level. Don't push the shoulder back too far. The power of the move comes from the controlled jab within your easy range of motion. With each jab make a sharp sound with your voice, the louder the better. FYI: The elbow block carries the energetics of the intention without risking damage to the elbow.*

*Follow this with a power kick sequence. If you are new to exercise, simply stomp on the floor as if you were stomping out a match. If you are* more advanced, kick by pushing through the heel from side to side. Do not snap or hyperextend your knee. Control the kick by stopping within the normal range of motion. Never kick so hard that you feel your knee lock or snap. Exhale as you kick, letting out a sharp sound with each kick.

After expressing your anger in this way, change your focus and change the movement. Ask yourself what lessons and wisdom this situation has to teach you. What grace can you call forth from your soul? From this place it becomes easier to move fluidly into the attitude of acceptance and blessing, as we did in chapter 1. This next step—signifying perseverance in the face of trouble—came to me when I was choreographing some music that honored Nelson Mandela. His life is an extraordinary example of turning spirit into action without holding on to bitterness and anger. This step symbolizes that we sow the seeds of change and then "keep on keeping on." Mandela did exactly this during twenty-seven years in prison. One can only guess at the moments of futility he must have experienced during all those years. Yet we never know how Divine Order will arrange the sequences of our lives. The lesson is to make our stand, release our anger, and persevere.

The perseverance step completes the process. Begin standing with feet hip-width apart and face the right. Take four steps to the right and with your hands make a gesture reminiscent of scattering seeds into the earth, with a slight bend at your hips. These are the seeds of your wisdom and

*your highest dreams for the world. Then step backward for three steps, adding a torso and chest wave with each step. This is a gesture of sending a prayer of blessing to the seeds of your vision. Then turn and repeat on the other side. Repeat for as long as it takes to internalize this mind-set. I will often do about twenty repetitions of this seed sowing.*

## Transforming Grief

Along with anger and fear, grief can be a stark, overwhelming emotion. When we are in the throes of deepest grief, movement can assist the process. Rocking back and forth is an almost universal motion of self-consolation that seems to come up naturally. At times we may have difficulty facing the depth of our grief for fear it will overwhelm us. Although we may know that crying is healthy and cathartic, we just don't want to go there again. But holding on to unresolved grief is deeply harmful to our psyches and prevents us from moving forward in life.

When I have difficulty resolving my grief, I go off by myself where I know I won't be disturbed. I sit quietly and begin to rock almost imperceptibly back and forth in a small motion while holding my heart. This motion spontaneously accompanies us when we cry and often unlocks the pain and allows us to feel it fully. We do have to feel our grief fully before we can let it go, so let the wisdom of the body guide the process.

Your goal in releasing any negative emotional energy is to return to your truest, most natural state of being, which is one of peace and balance, but it is up to you to get the energies moving. Intentional release and sacred movement are the fastest, most direct ways to unblock frozen emotions and open the process of healing.

## Freeing Stagnant Emotions

Other emotions besides anger, fear, and grief can become stuck inside us. Sometimes we find ourselves reluctant to express exuberant joy, feelings of love, or profound gratitude. It seems we're programmed to react when things go wrong, but we often forget to acknowledge "what's right" in our lives, or we're ashamed of the abandon the full expression of these emotions requires. Yet unexpressed feelings tend to stagnate inside us.

By moving to music, using gestures that express these emotions, you can give yourself permission to acknowledge that part of you. Bring all of yourself, just as you are, to the deep Presence that heals. In the movements that follow, it is safe to enter and express the wildness of your passion, confusion, and frustration. You don't need to deny or control these emotions. Through sacred movement, you can express them and use the wisdom of your spirit center to acknowledge and accept them.

# OTHER MOVEMENTS FOR EMOTIONAL SUPPORT

### ∼ For Emotional Balance ∼

*When you are feeling out of balance in your life, try this movement. Stand easily and feel the symmetry of your weight placed equally and balanced on both feet. With your arms extended out in front of you, trace the pattern of the yin/yang symbol or the infinity symbol, which looks like a figure eight on its side. Step side to side with your feet. Allow your torso to rotate comfortably along with your feet. Let the movement flow.*

### ∼ For Centering ∼

*If you find that you're having trouble getting centered and your thoughts are scattered, use this movement. First, take a deep breath and feel your feet connected to the earth. I like to do this to the sounds of a Native American flute, but you can do it silently, too. Open your hands wide as if you were embracing the chaos of a mind running wild. Bring your hands to the sides of your head, gathering your thoughts together, then begin to bring the energy of your focused attention down along the front of your body, connecting to the*

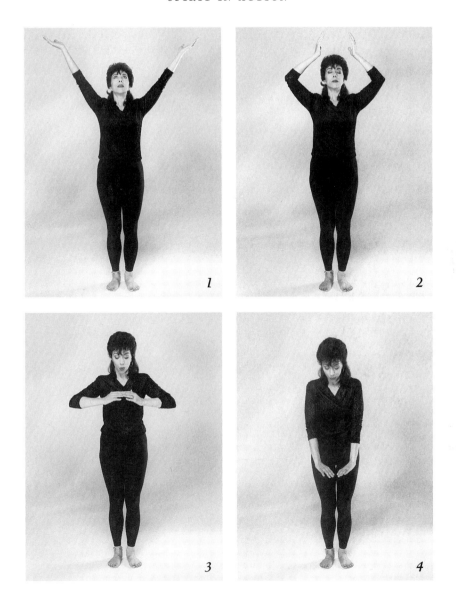

*earth, ending with your arms lowered, palms facing the earth. Repeat until you have come home to yourself. Typically I do one to ten repetitions.*

This exercise came in very handy during the shooting of my most recent videos, when I was surrounded by a dozen technical people but still had to stay centered in the prayerful dances so that the viewing audience would get drawn into sharing that quality. The other dancers and I had to work without distraction, so I found myself spontaneously doing the preceding exercise before each "take." The moving prayer helped keep my concentration clear and consistent during the hard twelve-hour day. The director commented on how the energy of the project and the energy of the technical crew seemed to flow at a higher-than-normal level throughout the day, so it seemed that my personal prayer affected the focus and flow of the people around me as well.

## ∼ For Breaking Up an Obsessive Thought ∼

*When we find our thoughts cycling in a pattern of worry or confusion, it means we are not in the present moment. We are focusing on an imagined future. To break this cycle and return to the present, I go to an old standby of mine: I get out my running shoes. I find that running or hiking vigorously (not a slow saunter) helps me to focus on the present. I try to go to a beautiful natural setting and focus on my feet hitting the ground one after the other. Get into the rhythm of the present and the rhythm of the breath. Sometimes I will chant "Ho" with each footstep, which helps to bring my attention to the earth—to the present. I make a point of ending my jaunt in a beautiful spot where I can meditate on the natural beauty around me and on the peace of this present moment.*

*If I'm running or hiking to overcome confusion or indecision, when I need an answer to a perplexing situation, I visualize a cord running from my solar plexus to a sacred place where I can find the solution to my situation. I allow the cord to pull me along, and I follow it as it brings me ever closer to Spirit and to the answer for my quest. This body prayer is an affirmation that the correct solution exists and that I will find it by allowing myself to be drawn deeply into the presence of Spirit.*

We are made of the stuff of stars, given our lives by a living world, given our selves by time. We are brother to the trees and sister to the sun. We are of such glorious stuff we need not carry pain around like a label. Our duty, as living things, [is] to be quite sure that pain is not our whole story, for we can choose to be otherwise. . . . We can choose to dance.

—SHERI S. TEPPLER, *SIX MOON DANCE*

# EXPANDING YOUR CHOICES
# AND RANGE OF POSSIBILITY

Giving full voice to all our emotions by embodying them can be frightening, especially if we were raised to contain and hide our emotions. Although the full complexity of passionate feelings may seem an unusual inclusion in a spiritual practice, wild or explosive feelings can be holy, too. The fullness of God, after all, includes the wildness of Creation.

Evidence of this wildness is all around us. Lightning flashes and thunder roars. Walls of water flood across the land. Gales of wind tear up everything in their path. Fires furiously consume huge swaths of forestlands. This is not the work of some polite Sunday school deity. This is the energy of transformation, changing all in its path. These are the energies of Shiva and Kali, deities often represented as the destructive face of Divinity, although these aspects represent the energies of change and the need for new growth. These forces are often frightening, but so are our own emotions. As we become more comfortable physically expressing the breadth of our emotions, however, we accelerate our growth into spiritual understanding and maturity.

# Part II

# AEROBIC
# PRAYERS

*Getting Started*

*"I Sing the Body Electric"*
—WALT WHITMAN

The way I design dances, retreats, and workshops comes out of my own spiritual practice as well as my twenty-two years as a chiropractor. Since my primary audiences are made up of "nondancers," I've created low-impact exercises that are safe and enjoyable. All movements in this book are inherently natural to the joints and muscles of your body.

When we move, the brain directs signals to various parts of the body through a series of nerve fibers originating in the spinal cord. Together, the brain and spinal cord make up the central nervous system of the body. This is computer central to the physical operating system of every major function of your body. The cranium houses the brain in a series of hard, protective bones. Likewise, the spinal vertebrae house the very delicate spinal cord, which sends nerve impulses to the functioning of the arms and hands, gastrointestinal tract, heart, lungs, legs, and feet, to name a few areas of the body.

The spine is the source of motion in the Aerobic Prayers. In a magnificent display of design, the spinal vertebrae are able to protect the cord and spinal nerves by a strong bony structure while maintaining a maximum range of fluid motion from segment to segment. The end result is that we have an amazing possibility of motion that originates in the core of the body, within the torso, facilitated by the motion of the spine. It is very important to maintain this gorgeous flexibility throughout our lifetime to ensure that we remain free of pain and in good health.

Many of my patients have come to me with poor, inflexible posture that requires me to "manipulate" the spinal column in order to reverse sloping shoulders and alleviate neck and/or lower-back pain. These "hands-on" treatments (*chiro* is Greek for "hands") correct aberrant motion of the joints, which can affect nerves, muscles, connective tissues, and organs.

The spine allows you to feel intimately connected to the spirituality within the dances. For example, if I tell you to step to the side and open your arms and your heart to the feeling of receiving a blessing, this movement is accompanied by extending the upper spine, which, in turn, expands the chest (metaphorically opening the heart) in coordination with the arms and feet. The spine is actually the primary facilitator of the feeling of heart connection in the dance.

On a metaphysical level the spinal cord represents the canal through which spiritual energy travels. In Eastern and Western meditation traditions, the spinal canal acts much like a divining rod that allows us to draw in energy and wisdom from above and connect this higher energy to the earth through conscious intention and right actions, or spirit in action. The spine is the vehicle through which our lives seed spiritual intention into the realm of the physical. It is the way that we, in concert with our Source, cocreate heaven on earth.

To open up the motion of the spine, I often include a number of movements that are not common to most people's daily habits. You will find a lot of circular motions to the hip and lower-back movements. These are facilitated by keeping your center of gravity low and along the plane of the earth as you step.

## ⌒ Loose Lower-Back Step ⌒

*Let's begin by taking a step forward and then back in place, with a lowered center of gravity. Begin standing naturally, with feet hip-width apart, arms hanging comfortably at your sides. Inhale and exhale three times and imagine bringing the breath into your spinal cord and out into the nerve-map of your body. When you're ready, bend your knees slightly, which will lower your weight a bit closer to the earth. Take a step forward with your right foot, leading with your heel, then step back. Visualize that you have a jug of water on your head and you don't want to spill a drop. Your hips can move side to side, but your head should not bob up and down. This frees up the lower back to move more fluidly and naturally. Reverse and step with your left foot for a few times, always focusing on a loose sway of the lower back and hips. The lower your center of gravity, the larger is the sway of the hips and lower back.*

## ∾ Movement for Loosening the Upper Body ∾

*I've borrowed liberally from a number of African traditions for movements for the upper spine. Several variations of a chest wave appear in some of the dances. Chest wave motion actually originates in the upper back, which extends and pushes the chest forward, and then flexes, pulling the chest in. This motion feels as if it were waking up your heart. When you pulse the chest open like this, it can feel as if you are pulsing your heart open.*

In addition to the spinal movement, I use a lot of large, expressive arm movements, which embody prayerful intention in most of the dances. These movements can make the dances aerobic, even though they are mostly nonimpact. By combining large, fluid arm movements with upper spinal motion, you will find that you develop a lot of upper body flexibility that carries into your everyday life. Some of my students have called it "regaining our wings." This expression describes a feeling of freedom in the upper body that is both physical and metaphorical. For me the only other exercise that stimulates that upper body freedom is swimming. This arm motion is especially beneficial for people who work in offices or at a computer a great deal. Our technological age has produced a population of workers who slump forward, with shoulders rounded and head jutting unnaturally forward of the spine. This not only looks bad but is also harmful to the stasis of the body's own "ecosystem." We've come to resemble question marks rather than following the straight, upright exclamation point of the spine!

Over time this habitual posture will begin to limit a normal, natural range of motion. The body was meant to move in a wide variety of ways throughout the day. When you inhibit this motion, you limit the feeling of freedom and well-being that is possible within your body. Chest waves and large arm movements that extend the shoulders, back, and neck support normal alignment and the natural grace with which we were meant to live. As an added benefit, many people find that when they use these programs, their chronic neck or back pain goes away.

## ～ Sitting Shoulder and Chest Roll ～

*Try this modified chest wave/shoulder roll when you find yourself stuck at your desk too long. While sitting, move your chair back about two feet from your desk. Take two or three deep breaths. Begin to roll your shoulders back and around in small circles. After five or six rolls, begin to bring your chest and upper back into the rolling motion. Continue for ten to fifteen more repetitions of this rolling, wavelike movement. I like to think of this as a mini–chest wave or "one-minute desk spa."*

# PUTTING SPIRIT IN ACTION

The following chapters are compilations of active prayers designed to give you a wide variety of explorations from which to adapt or create your own moving spiritual practice. If these moving meditations are done in their entirety, they also offer an excellent and safe way to get an aerobic workout. I have taught these movements to children, adults, and seniors as old as ninety-five.

The intensity of the aerobic component will depend on the energy you bring to the movements and on whether you use music or not. It will also depend on the music you choose. These exercises can all be done very slowly and deliberately (like tai chi) as well as vigorously (as in a step class) or at other tempos in between. You are in control of the pace that feels right to you. I have included a lot of selections in the "Musical Resources" section in the back of this book. Choose what you like, or you may want to move to an inner rhythm that suits you just fine.

The footwork is the least important aspect of these moving prayers. If you don't get the footwork right away, forget it for a while. It will come in the next session or two. I know what it is to take a class and be totally lost. If the footwork does not seem easy in some of the pieces, just relax and focus on your hands and arms. Everything will flow together with time. Stay centered in the prayer offered by each dance. Remember that the purpose of the footwork is to remind you of your connection to the earth. Nothing fancy is needed to maintain that grounded relationship. Feel free simply to step in place until you feel more comfortable.

You don't need a lot of space for Aerobic Prayer. An area as small as five feet by five feet will suffice. Once you begin to learn and remember your favorite dances, you can do them virtually anywhere. I have done the prayers to MTV in a hotel room when I'm traveling, and it works fine.

Some people have told me that they like to incorporate little rituals before they practice Aerobic Prayer, such as lighting a candle or incense. If this adds richness to your experience, if it helps to create a sacred space within your home and heart, I support it. It's one way in which sacred dance can influence your everyday life.

You don't need any special clothing, but you will most likely prefer to move in loose, comfortable clothes. Later on you may want to include props such as scarves or a flowing skirt just to see whether they change the feeling of the meditation and dance. I prefer to dance barefoot, but many people feel better moving in good supportive athletic shoes. Whatever you choose, remember, do not create a slippery surface. I strongly discourage you from wearing socks on a rug or bare floor because you could slip and hurt yourself. Please either go barefoot or wear shoes with nonslip soles.

If you choose to perform these dances as an aerobic exercise, please be sure to drink plenty of water to replace fluids lost through sweating. Keeping yourself hydrated also helps prevent injury.

The movements in each chapter are presented and described in the sequence that I find most natural and most effective in evoking a meditative state. You can do all or parts of the chapters, and you may find different combinations of movements that are good for you.

There are some general guidelines to consider if you are short on time and can do only part of a section. Be sure that you prepare your body for exercise with one of the warm-up sections. After a gentle warm-up, then move on to the dances that require higher energy. If you wish to create a regimen for yourself based on exercises from different chapters, remember that as the exercises proceed, they increase in vigor and intensity. Be smart when mixing movements so that you increase your heart rate in the safe way in which these movements were designed. Similarly, as you end your aerobic workout, follow any advanced exercises with one of the slower, cooldown dances or even by walking for a few minutes to return your heart rate to normal. Complete the session with some of the recommended stretches. If time allows, take a few moments for a silent or musical meditation to set the tone for the rest of your day.

The poems and song lyrics found after some of the dances in chapters 6 through 8 inspired the choreography. You may find that these words will further connect you to the dance, either before you begin or after you've completed prayerful movement. The choice to use them or not is yours. The "Musical Resources" section at the end of the book will enable you to locate the artist or poet.

A subsection called "Personal Explorations" follows most of the dances. These are optional exercises that need not be performed right after the main dance. Often a theme within one of the dances will strike a chord that you will want to explore a little deeper on some days, and these explorations will give you the material to do this. You'll find that most of these exercises are slower and more meditative than the aerobic dances and are meant to be explored independently from them. If you are trying to maintain an aerobic heart rate for a specific period of time, remember that you can come back to this material later in a quieter, more self-reflective time. The personal explorations also give you exercises that stand alone as moving meditations for days when you simply don't have the physical vitality to do the dances that require more energy.

Clear focus and intention are the keys to capturing the essence of each movement. Let your hands carry your intention and let your eyes focus on your hands. This attention to your body develops the moving mantras and will distract your busy mind from its usual chatter. When your intention combines with deep awareness of your movements, you are joining together body, mind, and spirit.

# A NOTE FOR THOSE WITH LIMITED MOBILITY

Since most of the prayerful action comes from the focused arm and hand gestures, the Aerobic Prayer practices can be easily adapted for use by people with limited mobility in the lower part of their body. Remember that following your hand and arm movements with your eyes adds energy and a sense of purpose to the gestures.

Adapting the movements for elderly people is likewise easily accomplished. If the footwork seems too complicated, let it go. Simply march in place or do no foot movements at all. The arm gestures throughout Part II are shown as large movements. If you are new to expressing yourself through movement, make the motions smaller, keeping the elbows no higher than shoulder height.

• • •

The most important part of praying with our bodies is keeping the spirit of prayer alive and strong and opening our hearts to the Holy Spirit of Oneness. As long as there is breath in our bodies, we each have the opportunity to express our lives as a dance of the sacred path.

# Chapter 5

# EXPLORATIONS—
# SINGS MY SOUL

Let's begin to put spirit in action with a series of moving meditations that represent a wide diversity of spiritual explorations. These prayers will help you find balance, develop harmony in your life, and celebrate the cycles of nature. This is a good place to start, whether you're a beginner to movement or you consider yourself fit, because these movements are welcoming and gentle. The music I recommend is instrumental, and the prayer and reflections are verbal cues for you, the dancer, to utilize or change to suit your own mood. Sometimes a movement will mean something different to you than what I suggest. Feel free to explore any of the themes in this chapter in a way that is true for you. This leaves you lots of freedom to create your own personalized embodied prayers with music that suits your taste and your energy level on a given day.

## INVOKING SPIRIT

These beginning movements are designed to warm up the body gently. Our *intention* is to call ourselves to spiritual *attention*. The body is the house of the spirit: we're about to open the windows and doors. The most universal themes in sacred dance are reaching up to an image of Spirit that is metaphorically above us or of dropping into center and reaching for the flame of Spirit within

us. To begin movement, my preference is to lengthen and extend the body by reaching above. If this conflicts with your personal theology, I always encourage you to experiment and find the way that works for you.

~

INTENTION: *I invite higher awareness to my mind, body, and spirit to-day. As I gently warm up my body, I feel new energy being fluidly released throughout my inner and outer being.*
MUSIC: *Instrumental, flowing, soft rhythms.*
EXERCISE: *Warm-up.*

Begin with your feet shoulder-width apart. Reach to the sky (ceiling) with alternating hands as an internal call to Spirit. Repeat three times. Repetitions help add gestures to the body's physical memory bank, so that you can call on these gestures later on, no matter where you are. The first physical call invites the Holy Spirit of Life to be with us in mind. Allow your hands to drift down to the front of your thighs so that your hands are now supporting the weight of your torso. This is fol-

lowed by eight low-back releases. The small of the back is raised and lowered eight times. This gently loosens the lower spine, where so many of us store tension as well as physical/spiritual knots.

The second "call" of arm reaches overhead affirms our awareness that we are part of and have our being in this Sacred Source. This is followed again by eight low-back releases.

Again, reach overhead three times. The third call invites the Sacred Source into our bodies in the form of vitality, health, and energy. Again, follow with eight back releases.

Come back to your starting (neutral) position. Roll your shoulders eight times forward, then reverse and roll them eight times in the opposite direction. The rolling of the shoulders forward is akin to sending spirit out into the world, whereas the opposite movement can be considered a gathering of spirit. What we put out in the world is often what we receive back.

Next, step to the right side, reach to the right, and step together. Go to your left side and reach left, allowing a long, elegant stretch in the spine and ribs. Repeat eight times. As you feel your body warm up and loosen, appreciate this energy as a gift of Spirit.

Continue to sidestep to alternating sides two times and then add four rolling pulses of the chest and spine. This is a wavelike movement of your spine and rib cage. If you can, comfortably bend slightly forward toward the earth as you pulse (wave) your chest and upper spine. This movement is a way to stimulate a sense of opening your heart to send a blessing directly from the heart. In this case, you are going to use the movement as a blessing of gratitude to the gifts you experience from Creation.

Next, go back to the side step and reach above your head again with alternating hands to a count of four. As you do this, celebrate the warmth of the sun with the reaching motion. Now add the four heart pulses toward the earth with gratitude for the gifts of the sweet earth.

Reach and step to your side as just described, celebrating the beauty of the moon. Let the heart pulse again for the rhythms of the earth.

Reach and step to your side again, celebrating the mystery of the stars. Let the heart pulse this time for the rhythms and cycles of our lives.

Continue this step sequence, finding your own elements of creation to celebrate with the heart pulses. Find the prayer that comes from within your own body and dance it. This invocation of spirit allows you to continue on with spirit in action, adding more prayerful movements to your physical and spiritual vocabulary.

# LET ME BE A DIVINE INSTRUMENT

The next theme in this series of dances begins with the prayer that we may become an instrument of Divine purpose in the way that we live our lives. Every time we choose mindful, right action, every time we adopt an attitude of peace, every time we extend our help to another, we act as the force of good in the world. This makes us a conscious vehicle of Divine intention and purpose. This dance serves to expand our awareness of being carriers of light in our world. In it we are encouraged to explore how it is we may serve in our own world.

How do you express Divine purpose in your life? Is it a smile for a stranger? Is it actively listening to a friend in need? Have you encouraged a young person? In this next dance ask how you can be a light in your world today. At work. At home. To strangers. To loved ones. In ways that no one will ever see.

Every time we express kindness, every time we are willing to extend forgiveness, every time we act with compassion, we express Spirit on earth. With hands raised in the next dance, we ask that our actions be instruments for peace and wholeness. With hands lowered, we imagine that we are spreading Divine purpose in the world. As we repeat the pattern, we begin to internalize the prayer, exploring how we may personally actualize these qualities.

~

INTENTION: *May my life be a vehicle to express my spirit and the One Spirit.*
MUSIC: *Soft jazz, lightly rhythmic tropical island, New Age rhythmic.*
EXERCISE: *Aerobic.*

In a neutral starting position, we'll begin with a box step, sometimes called a jazz square. Cross your right foot in front of the left. Then cross your left foot in front of the right. Then step back to the starting position with your right foot and back to the starting position with the left foot. Repeat the footwork pattern ten times before switching feet. Now lead with the left for ten repetitions.

When your feet cross in front of each other, your hands lift above your head with palms open. This gesture demonstrates an attitude of receptivity to Divine inspiration and purpose.

The next gesture is done as the feet step back one at a time. Your hands

come down with palms down, as if you were spreading around to your world the guidance and blessings you have received.

As you begin to understand the personal ways that you express the Divine Source in your world, notice how your body comes alive in the dance. It is a joyful privilege to participate in the creation of wholeness and healing.

Repeat this pattern ten to sixty times. Change your lead leg every ten repetitions or so for musculoskeletal balance. Let your body dance this prayer!

There is a break step in this dance to give your muscles a change in the moving mantra.

With the next step we remember that we are surrounded by spiritual gifts such as peace and grace at every moment, though we often forget these gifts, believing that we are separated from the Divine Source and acceptance. With this part of the dance, we acknowledge that we are surrounded by gifts of Spirit always. Receive them fully as the waterfall quenches your thirst on a hot, parched day. What are those gifts you wish to accept today? Peace? Joy? Courage? Abundance?

~

INTENTION: *I remember to receive ____ with every breath I take.*

Starting from neutral position, step right-left-right, moving toward your right while facing front, then left-right-left, moving toward the left. Your hands are lifted, palms up, toward the direction to which you are traveling. It is as if the hands were catching drops of rain from a sun shower on an August afternoon. Repeat ten to forty times. Let your body dance your prayer. When you feel refreshed and replenished and are ready to end the movement, return to neutral position. Raise your hands once more to receive Divine Energy and lower them, palms down, below your waist to affirm your initial intention of being an instrument of spiritual oneness.

# EXPLORING BALANCE

Our next moving mantra is an embodied exploration of what it means to live in balance. First, we'll explore our physical boundaries of balance. The altered physical sense of balance in this next dance is a wonderful metaphor for the dips, turns, and about-faces with which we have to contend in life. No one gets out of this life without having to deal with difficulties and challenges that often leave us feeling off balance. We may even sometimes feel as if we are falling. It's important to choose to create our own movements to break our emotional fall. We can move on through these feelings that threaten to drag us down. We can maintain a spiritual center that helps us keep in motion. We can learn to dance through our lessons without judgment or attachment. Herein lie the tests to our faith in the larger wisdom of life.

When your mind and emotions are a boat rocking at sea, trust the wisdom of your body to help you find your balance, in spite of the waters roiling around you. The movement of this dance reminds us that when we remain spiritually grounded, we retain our sense of balance. Sometimes life feels like waves of instability, so learn to surf and have fun anyway. Let the current bring you home.

~

INTENTION: *I remain balanced and grounded regardless of my outer circumstances.*
MUSIC: *Rhythmic, fairly fast. Caribbean and Brazilian work well with these steps.*
EXERCISE: *Aerobic.*

Face to your right. Take three steps to the right, starting with the left foot. With your weight still on your left foot, take a turn on the ball of your foot that allows you to bring yourself around to face your left. A small hop while turning will help you make the change in direction. Repeat the sequence now facing left: beginning with the right foot, hop and turn on your right foot again facing right. The arms and hands are out to the sides as a kind of rudder to the turns. Repeat this pattern fifteen to twenty times. Feel free to double-time it when you become comfortable with the movement. If the hop turn is difficult for you, just take four steps forward and back.

Once you understand the pattern, begin to play with your balance by moving your torso slightly forward of your usual balance point. You may feel as

if you were just short of falling forward into the movement. You see this subtle addition of loose balance play in the samba. Experiment with your own range of play here.

The second step in this prayer comes from the Caribbean islands. Its history goes back to the days when the slaves on the plantations were kept in one leg iron to prevent escape, as described in chapter 2. Even with the enormity of their suffering and abuse, they found the courage and the dignity of spirit to dance. Even though it was prohibited, they danced their pain and their hopes for the future. Can we find it in our hearts to do the same with our own sorrows?

With your left foot as your pivot foot, begin to turn clockwise (backward) around this foot for a count of eight. Then change feet and pivot in a circle around the other foot. As you pivot backward, play again with balance as you learn to adjust for the feeling of instability. Repeat this eight to ten times.

Return once more now to the original three steps to the side, followed by the hop turn. End this dance at the natural conclusion of your music or whenever your body says to end. Exhale and inhale deeply and become aware of your breath. Feel the ground beneath your feet. Repeat the intention: "I remain balanced and grounded regardless of my outer circumstances." Through balance, we acknowledge that whatever it is we think we want, life always gives us what best fosters the growth of our soul.

### PERSONAL EXPLORATION

This is one of the hatha yoga postures that help to develop physical balance and mental concentration. During this practice affirm that you are becoming more whole and balanced every day.

There are several ways of doing this, depending on your ability and experience. In the beginning be sure that you do this with a wall or chair nearby, in case you need to hold on to something for stability. First, stand up straight. Pick a point on which to fix the attention of your eyes. Lift the chest and bring the hands to prayer position, elbows out. Place the underside of one foot just above the other ankle, knee open, and hold. Breathe. If you can, try to bring the foot up to rest on the inside of the thigh. As you advance, raise the foot to the upper inner thigh.

Switch sides and repeat at your comfort level. Your sense of balance may change. Many people notice that at first it's easier to balance on the dominant leg, but with persistence, the weak side becomes as adept as the stronger one.

# REVERENCE AND GRATITUDE

When we practice gratitude, we are by definition living in the present moment. When we practice gratitude, we are practicing acceptance. This next dance offers another opportunity to practice gratitude through movement.

⌒

INTENTION: *I am filled with gratitude for the goodness in my life.*
MUSIC: *Rhythmic, flowing, soft jazz, cool Latin, rhythmic New Age music.*
EXERCISE: *Aerobic.*

In this next step, when you raise your arms in reverence, consider the beauty of Creation laid before you. Use this gesture to honor the beauty of these gifts. Joseph Campbell once said that every time we sigh at the beauty of a sunset or the majesty of a mountain, we are praying. (Think how often you've prayed without really knowing it.) In that moment we are appreciating Creation and the Holy Source of all things. Let this dance express all that touches your heart. Is it holding a baby in your arms? Is it the desert in bloom? Is it the quiet whisper of snow in the pines? Find your own prayer and let your body pray it with deep reverence.

We begin with a mambo step. Starting in a neutral position, step front with your right leg, then step back with the same foot. As you step front and back, keep your knees bent more than usual. This loosens the hips and lower back as you step. It gives your pelvis a sense of moving horizontally along the plane of the earth.

As you step forward, raise the hands above the head as a gesture of reverence. Lower the arms on the back step. This is the entire pattern—front and back. Change the lead foot about every eight to ten repetitions. I will often re-

peat this pattern fifty to one hundred times, naming as many gifts of wonder and beauty as I can think of.

In the second step in the dance, surrender even deeper to the movement and name those things for which you are grateful today. Let your eyes follow your hands, adding intention to the prayer. Change the step slightly by stepping your right foot to the right side and back, then the left foot to the left side and back. As you step to the side, open your arms to the side. As you open your arms, open your heart in gratitude and name all the personal blessings of your life. Change the lead foot again every eight to ten repetitions. End this dance at the natural conclusion of the music or whenever your body feels complete with the movement. This life-affirming dance is one of my favorites.

## PERSONAL EXPLORATION

All too often in life, we are not fully aware of the people and things that hold deep meaning for us until they are taken from us. It is as if we do not truly feel the importance of these values on a day-to-day basis because of our chronic inattention and busyness. Consistently taking the time to honor that for which we are grateful keeps us in touch with the reality of what we have in the here and now. I am often awed by the deep emotion that comes up in workshops and classes I teach when the participants take the time to remember what they hold most dear.

What follows is a very quiet prayer of gratitude that can be done to conclude this exploration or practiced in place of the preceding more vigorous version. Simply touch your heart with the thought of gratitude and lift the hands in acknowledgment to the Creator Source. This can be repeated as long as you wish to a defined musical beat or in the deepest rhythm of all: silence.

## CLOSER AND CLOSER—A DANCE OF DEVOTION

### "MY BELOVED"

Know that my beloved is hidden from everyone
Know that she is beyond the beliefs of all beliefs
Know that in my heart she is as clear as the moon
Know that she is the life in my body and in my soul

—RUMI

This next dance comes from a devotional practice. You can accompany it with the following beautiful chant, which speaks of God as the Beloved, often heard in the ecstatic poetry of Rumi: "Closer and closer, each step to my Beloved.

God, you're in each breath I take. You are my Beloved." (This chant comes from Scott Kalechstein's song "Closer and Closer," listed in the "Musical Resources" section at the back of the book.) It is, of course, not necessary to use this music. Use whatever music has a rhythm that allows you to work comfortably with the movement that will be described.

~

INTENTION: *"God, you're in each breath I take. You are my Beloved."*
MUSIC: *"Closer and Closer," by Scott Kalechstein, from the* CD *Eyes of* **God,** *or any soft, rhythmic, evocative music.*
EXERCISE: *Aerobic.*

Hands bring depth to this body prayer. Begin in a neutral position. One at a time, reach your hands above your head and invite the sense of Spirit into your heart area. Then reach with both hands to your heart and move them up along your upper body; extend the "breath of God" from your heart into your throat area. Release your hands upward once more, as if you were exhaling a gift from your own mouth, as a flower that is lifted in offering to the Beloved. This is a beautiful metaphor for offering your life as your prayer.

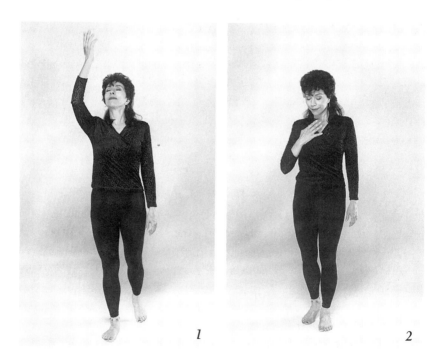

1                              2

Now for the feet. Begin in neutral position with your feet shoulder-width apart. Step your right foot behind, then step back to your starting position. Repeat the pattern on your other side, right foot behind and then back.

This is the complete pattern repeated as mantra. As in all movement, let your eyes follow your hands to add intention to the prayer. Come to completion at the natural end of the music or when your body begins to signal fatigue. Stay in stillness for a moment, taking a deep breath and enjoying the sense of intimacy with the Divine that this moving mantra brings up.

## A DANCE OF PETITION

Some people say that the first step on the spiritual path is "O God, please help me!" and the final prayer at the end of our spiritual journey is "Thank you for everything." Of course, there are a great many nuances in between, not the least of which is "God, if you do [whatever], I'll never do [whatever] again." This is a kind of spiritual "Let's make a deal." It is a very good thing that the Cosmos has a sense of humor, or we all would have been smitten down generations ago.

The next dance offers a prayer of petition, which combines affirmation, visualization, faith, and acceptance of a Higher Will to which we may not be privy. In this dance we lift up the person for whom we are praying or the situation about which we are praying out of the difficulty with the first part of our movement. As we bring the image of the person through the heart center, we hold him or her as healed, whole, and in the perfect love of the Great Spirit. Then we carry that vision and intention of wholeness as the offering to the Source of all healing, comfort, and peace. See it as done.

INTENTION: *I hold _____ as healed and whole and residing in the perfect love of the Great Spirit.*
MUSIC: *Flowing, rhythmic; soft jazz; New Age rhythmic.*
EXERCISE: *Aerobic.*

Here's the embodiment of the prayer. Begin in a neutral position. Cross your right foot in front, turning your body toward the left. While facing the side, let your right hand reach down as if you were scooping up the issue of your attention. Then step back to center, carrying the item up through the midline of your torso to overhead. Remember to let your eyes follow your hand. Continue for thirty to forty repetitions.

Change sides now and continue for thirty to forty repetitions. Create as many different prayers as you wish or stay in the same prayer for the entire session.

In the second step we surrender to the will of Spirit. Part of our human experience is to do the work of cleaning up our thoughts and hold positive intentions. After that we also know that there are times when we have to learn to release our visualization and learn acceptance.

The second embodied prayer in the piece acknowledges the need to release and surrender. Begin facing to your left in neutral position. Step forward with your right foot while extending your hands down in front of your body with palms open. Step back with hands up. Again step forward, releasing your hands in front. Then come back to center, facing front with your hands to the heart. Repeat in the other direction. Release and surrender. Repeat the sequence twenty to fifty times, alternating sides. Conclude this dance by coming to stillness in neutral position. Affirm: "I hold _____ in healing and wholeness and in the right place for the highest good to work through his or her soul."

## PERSONAL EXPLORATION

This exercise comes from a simple yet very powerful prayer for surrender and acceptance used in some cloistered communities. If it is made with an attitude of sincere spiritual surrender, it can evoke a truly transformational effect.

At times we have enormous difficulty accepting what life has given us. We may suffer profound grief, the loss of a child or spouse, rage from betrayal, the catastrophic loss of our worldly goods. These are the life events that can leave us feeling as if we just could not go on. Life's vicissitudes seem too great to

bear. We are in a stuck place that appears to have no way out. Our very soul is crying out in despair.

Simply lie facedown on the floor with your forehead to the floor, arms spread out to the sides, shoulder level, palms down. The phrase "Thy will, not mine" acts as the intention. This is a deep, embodied prayer of surrender. It is powerful because it acknowledges that we cannot find the answers to everything in our heads. Decide to trust that the reasons for what is will be revealed in Spirit's time, not ours. It is one of the hardest things we have to face as humans.

To be able to move into healing, we must first accept where we are. Remember the circle of spiritual understanding and that only from acceptance can healing take place. Healing asks us to transform radically, and of course, we fear that we are simply not up to the task. When you feel most broken, however, come to surrender. The easiest place to begin is by trusting that your body will lead your mind to healing. When your heart is broken, trust that it is Spirit cracking it open to receive the light of the soul in a deeper way. You are being transformed. You are being made new.

Whenever possible, perform this simple embodied prayer outside on the earth, weather permitting. Contacting the earth with your body helps you remember the ways in which the earth herself transforms on an ongoing basis. Ask that all the places that are not in alignment with your spiritual unfolding be taken into the earth and transmuted. To end this prayer, slowly lift yourself to sitting or standing position, inhale and exhale slowly and deeply three times, and say, "Teach me to be an instrument of change where I can be and to be accepting when it is necessary."

*Note:* This exercise can be done at any time. If it is done at a time of crisis, it is often very cathartic and may elicit tears and sobs. Tears are a beautiful, sacred part of our humanity and our healing, so let them come fully. They are a way of pouring out the depths of our grief. They are a cleansing gift of Spirit and a blessing. If you are outside, allow your tears to fall on the earth as a gift to be returned as wisdom.

# THE DANCE OF SELF-REFLECTION
## (THE DANCE OF THE CHAKRAS)

This dance helps us find ways to express right action and harmony in our lives and the world by activating the power of the seven energy centers in the body called chakras. These centers correspond to physical, emotional, and spiritual aspects of our being. By focusing on these centers, we can discover new energy for mindful living.

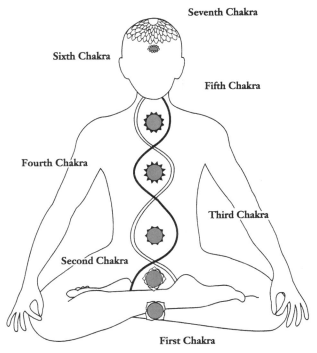

*The Seven Energy Centers, or Chakras*

~

INTENTION: *My life is a reflection of harmony.*
MUSIC: *Rhythmic, flowing; New Age rhythmic.*
EXERCISE: *Aerobic.*

The step is simple. Begin in neutral position. Place your right foot behind your left, then return it to neutral. (Note: When you become more advanced, you may want to add a quick cha-cha step between sides.) On the step behind, gather grace with your hands into the area of each of the chakras. On the step back to neutral, open the hands to manifest this grace out into the world. Because there is a lot to remember with the different levels in this dance, you might prop up or post a list that helps you remember the levels during the dance.

Start with your hands low, gathering grace at the level of the base of the spine. This area signifies the foundations of your life. This chakra contains the emotional energy that surrounds issues of safety and security, including emotions and energy related to career, job security, or where you live. Does your home feel like a safe haven? Is there anything that has to do with foundations and security that you need to address today? Continue to gather grace into this area, and when you are ready, express or move it out into your surroundings.

Next, move the hands to gather energy into the level of the lower abdomen. This is the center of creativity. What gifts of creativity want expression through you today? Creativity can include a way to solve a problem at work or to heal a relationship as well as a desire to write or paint or dance. Let the sense of creativity naturally flow from you.

Now bring the hands and your awareness up to the level of the solar plexus. This area has to do with issues of power and its complement, acceptance. Is there a place in your life in which you need to assert yourself? Perhaps you are struggling with an issue in which you need to give up controlling behavior. Continue to bring grace to this place in your life. Let the body lead you into the exploration.

Next, bring the hands and awareness up to the level of the heart. Open your heart with the movement and ask, "Who needs my love most today?" Is it a friend, a child, a spouse? Is it yourself? Where is your love needed most today? Act upon your inner direction.

Now move your hands to the area of the throat and pray for the grace of clear communication. Is there a truth that needs to be spoken to yourself or to someone else that you have been avoiding? Is there a need to express yourself eloquently today? Focus on the ability to speak what is truly in your heart.

Now bring the hands up to the level of the eyes, which is traditionally the third eye, just above the eyes and in the center of the forehead. Pray here for clear guidance. Ask that you may see clearly right action that needs to be taken in your life.

Next, bring your hands just above the crown of the head. Pray here for spiritual wisdom to light your path and inspire you deeply. May you see the light and love of Spirit reflected in the faces of all you meet today.

Now circle the hands around the body. In doing this, you express the fullness of all seven areas of your life. When all seven energy centers are working

together, we are living in harmony. We pray that Divine Harmony blesses us deeply and blesses the earth. As you end this dance, lower your palms to face the ground, sending your blessing of harmony to the earth and to all beings residing on her.

# WALKING ON HOLY GROUND

~

INTENTION: *I am walking on holy ground wherever I am.*
MUSIC: *"You Guide Me," by Scott Kalechstein, from the CD* Eyes of God*, or rhythmic New Age music.*
EXERCISE: *Cooldown.*

The cooldown gently returns the heart rate to resting. It's always recommended that after you complete aerobic activity, you take a few minutes to allow your body to recover. You can do this to music, as illustrated here, or practice in silence.

As you begin the movement, become aware of the ground beneath your feet. Begin to step in place. With this step we acknowledge that Divine Presence is everywhere. This means that we are stepping on Holy Ground this in-

stant and every instant. Because this Presence is everywhere, then all the people we meet today, we meet on Holy Ground. May we see on all the faces we meet today the Divine Light in yet another disguise and may we treat one another accordingly. With these thoughts in mind, begin to walk softly in any pattern you wish.

As you continue to take your steps, imagine that you are leaving the footprints of your life on this Holy Ground. Will they be footprints of stress, hurry, and anxiety? Or will they be footprints of joy and serenity? What prints can you leave in your life today? Let the steps you leave create a path of beauty behind you.

As you continue to walk around the room, make small circles with your shoulders to relax into the grounded movement. Keep your hands open, palms up. Keep your heart open as well.

Now find your own rhythm and step. Move in any way you desire. Let the wisdom of your body guide you. Breathe deeply and evenly.

Here are the words from the song that inspired this movement:

### "YOU GUIDE ME"

You guide me wherever I go.
Step by step, Lord, you're leading me home.
Like a stream in the desert,
Like a path through the snow,
Wherever I am in this world,
You're guiding me home.

—SCOTT KALECHSTEIN

## STRETCHES

When doing stretches, try them with your favorite slow music. My preference is often very soft music without lyrics or a defined beat. It is good to relax during the stretches. As with the preceding cooldown, I recommend that you take the time to stretch your muscles after performing aerobic activity.

Begin by sitting on the floor with one leg extended out to the side comfortably and the other bent with the foot to the groin. When stretching your hamstrings (back of the thigh) on the floor, it is always better to bend one knee.

This protects the lower back. Sitting up straight, with a flat back, facing front, press your chest forward until you feel the stretch in your inner thigh. The goal is not to press the chest to the floor, which can be hard on the lower back, but to press forward just until you feel the stretch in the inner thigh.

Next, turn and face the foot that is flexed upward. Again, with a tall, flat back, press the chest toward the foot, not the knee, until you feel the stretch in the back of the thigh. Hold and relax. Try not to bounce. If you cannot relax into the stretch, you are forcing too hard. Lighten up. Stretching should feel good.

If you are stretching your right hamstrings, place your left hand on the floor just behind your left hip. Pressing your weight into the left hand and opposite heel, lift your hips off the floor and reach overhead with your right hand. This contracts the hamstrings. Relax back to the floor and once more press the chest toward the foot. Notice how your flexibility has increased slightly after the reach. This is called antagonistic stretching. It is a very powerful aid in convincing the muscles to relax. Once more, reach and press into the heel and opposing hand. Relax and stretch once more.

Next, turn and face the floor with your left knee flexed and your right leg extended behind you. Rotate your torso so that your weight is on the right hip, not on the flexed knee. The weight is also supported on the hands. Allow gravity to rotate the extended hip into the floor. Hold for about ten seconds.

This stretches the front of the thigh and the front of the hip, which is particularly good if you sit all day at work. The hip is in contraction for long periods of time. This counteracts that contraction.

For a more advanced stretch of the quadriceps (front of the thigh), you can reach behind and hold the ankle for ten seconds.

If you have difficulty with this stretch, an alternative stretch is to lie on your side and hold on to the ankle as shown. This also stretches the front of the thigh. If your flexibility is such that this is difficult, begin by using a towel, as demonstrated. Make the stretch enjoyable. There is no need to contort your spine trying to do something as pictured when your body desires another approach. There is no "one way" to stretch any more than there is "one way" to God.

For a complete refreshing of the body, and for balance, repeat the preceding sequence on your other side.

 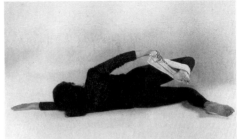

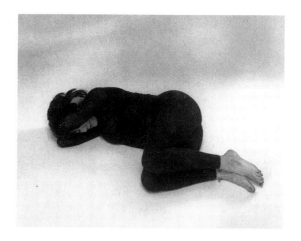

Next, lie down on your side, knees drawn up, almost in fetal position. Your hands are behind your head, with elbows in front of your face. Take in a deep breath. As you exhale, allow the top elbow to unwind so it opens up to the opposite side of the floor. This is a delicious stretch. Hold and take three deep breaths in this position. The breath itself will "massage" the spine in a gentle way.

Lift your top knee, followed by your other knee. Slowly turn to the other side and repeat.

With these relaxing stretches, you should be ready now to lie in a comfortable position to enjoy a musical meditation.

# MUSICAL MEDITATION

~

MUSIC: *Any soft, relaxing, flowing music of your choice.*
EXERCISE: *Relaxation/meditation.*

Find the most comfortable position for you. Relax and breathe deeply and fully. Let yourself deepen into the music. Let your breath be full. Let your thoughts be still. Imagine that the music is washing over you and through you, washing away any tension or negativity. Repeat the following: "I rest in spirit."

Take this affirmation with you into your day. Enjoy!

# Chapter 6

# NATIVE SPIRIT: PRAYERFUL DANCES WITH NATIVE AMERICAN THEMES

*I, I am the spirit within the earth.*
*The feet of the earth are my feet;*
*The legs of the earth are my legs.*
*The strength of the earth is my strength;*
*The thoughts of the earth are my thoughts;*
*The voice of the earth is my voice.*
*The feather of the earth is my feather;*
*All that surrounds the earth surrounds me.*
*I, I am the sacred works of the earth.*
*It is lovely indeed, it is lovely indeed.*
    —"SONG OF THE EARTH SPIRIT,"
    NAVAJO ORIGIN LEGEND, FROM
    *EARTH PRAYERS FROM AROUND*
    *THE WORLD*, EDITED BY
    ELIZABETH ROBERTS AND
    ELIAS AMIDON

This set of prayers uses rhythms and movements from several indigenous traditions, and many of my musical recommendations include Native American rhythms and themes.

Before we begin any of the directed movements, however, I suggest that you read the words to the following song. They are a powerful reminder that we are sacred, strong expressions of Spirit, and as such, we are capable of great acts. The lyrics were written as an affirmation that invites women to see their own beautiful, feminine energy as a unique manifestation of the Divine. Men should feel free to replace the gender-specific pronouns in this song to celebrate their own spiritual beauty.

"I AM ENOUGH"

I am enough, I am enough
Just as I am.
I am enough,
Just as I am, just as I am.
I am enough,
Just as I am.

I am a woman, I am a woman.
My body's sacred.
I am a woman.
My body's sacred, my body's sacred
I am a woman
My body's sacred.

In God's own image, in God's own image
I am created
In God's own image;
I am created, I am created,
In God's own image,
I am created.

I'm standing strong, I'm standing strong.
I won't be moved.
I'm standing strong.
I won't be moved, I won't be moved
I'm standing strong.
I won't be moved.

I am enough, I am enough.
I walk in beauty
I am enough.

I walk in beauty, I walk in beauty,
I am enough
I walk in beauty.

—COLLEEN FULMER

## KISS OF SPIRIT

The first moving prayer in this series encourages us to open our hearts to the gifts of Spirit, which abound around us. The words to the song that follows the movements inspired this gentle opening movement. The images remind us of earth, air, fire, and water, the elements of the life matrix that supports us. Kiss of Spirit teaches us to be present in the beauty of this moment. The movements gently prepare the body for more vigorous activity. This is a lovely prayer with which to begin your day.

~

INTENTION: *I open my mind and body to the present moment. I receive the goodness around me as a "kiss of spirit."*
MUSIC: *"Kiss of Spirit," by Cathie Malach and Kim Rosen, from the* CD Delphys: Ocean Born, *or music with light and flowing rhythms.*
EXERCISE: *Warm-up.*

Whenever you are warming up, it's always a good idea to check in quietly with yourself and see which areas especially want to be stretched today. Begin with your feet shoulder-width apart. Make three gentle arm circles, warming up the shoulders, followed by alternating reaches overhead. The three full arm circles act as a call to awaken body, mind, and spirit. The alternating reaches above the head remind us to reach for our highest values today and open up movement in the shoulders, chest, and upper back while lengthening the entire spine.

Next, reach side to side at shoulder level with palms up. This action matches the lyrics in the song, "Receive the Kiss of Spirit," in all of the many and wondrous manifestations in our lives. You are reaching out to the elements of earth, air, fire, and water—all gifts of Spirit—and asking to receive them in your life today. You are saying that you will be awake and receptive to their beauty. What are the gifts to which you want to be open and receptive today?

*Arm circle*  Alternating reaches

*Alternating side reaches*

The above movements stretch the upper back and chest. Bring your hands to the front, palms away from you at shoulder level. Clasp hands and press away to the front, stretching your upper back. Now reach behind you with arms outstretched and clasp your hands. If you find it difficult to clasp your hands, hold a towel or cloth between your hands instead. There's no need to push yourself. If stretching doesn't feel good, you are probably trying too hard.

We stretch the calves, hips, and hamstrings with the next series of

*Calf stretch*

stretches. Begin by stepping back on the right leg, keeping the heel down, stretching the right calf. Extend your arms at shoulder level a little wider than 45 degrees, palms up, being open to the kiss of Spirit. Hold for several seconds. Next, bend the left knee forward while your back leg stays straight. Your heel may come off the floor. This stretches the front of the right hip. Next, bend the right knee and straighten the left knee. Flatten the lower back and support your weight on the left thigh. This stretches the hamstring behind the left thigh. Repeat this series of leg stretches on the other side. Be patient with your body, especially if you are a beginner at this form of movement.

End the sequence the way you began it, with three full arm circles, opening the heart and chest. Hold the intention of surrendering to the Spirit around and within.

### "KISS OF SPIRIT"

Receive the kiss of Spirit from the Rock
her ancient heart will always talk
to one who remembers.

Receive the kiss of Spirit from the Breath
a constant flow of life and death
a path of surrender.

Receive the kiss of Spirit from the Fire
her flames are leaping ever higher
for one who remembers.

Receive the kiss of Spirit from the Flow
of water blessing head to toe
the path of surrender.

Receive the kiss of Spirit from the Earth
O sacred passageway of birth
for one who remembers.

Receive the kiss of Spirit from the Sea
her salty tears will set you free:
the path of surrender.

Receive the kiss of Spirit from the Sky
awaken to the eagle's cry
to one who remembers.

Receive the kiss of Spirit from within
the kiss that calls you to begin
the path of surrender.

—CATHIE MALACH AND KIM ROSEN

## PERSONAL EXPLORATION

Find any music that you especially enjoy, or see my suggestions in the "Musical Resources" section at the end of the book. Allow your body to move to the music and hold your attention on the theme of Kiss of Spirit. Ask yourself now, "To what do I want to be more receptive? What movement can my body create that makes me feel more open, vulnerable, and receptive?"

How is life asking me to learn acceptance? What movements allow me to feel that I am embracing those elements in my life? How can I learn to live in the present? What movement brings me clarity and focus on the present moment and on the sacredness of the eternal now?

There is great wisdom stored in your body. It can be trusted. It will lead you as you become more open to allowing it a voice of its own. Remember, you are in your own environment. There is no wrong way to dance. You need only to become aware in body, mind, and spirit.

# THE MAGIC OF RELATIONSHIPS

In the previous dance we opened to the present moment by acknowledging the beauty of the natural world. Here, we'll be moving with the knowledge that personal relationships help us to grow. This prayerful dance was inspired by the song "Magic," written by Nan Collie. It celebrates the healing transformations that accompany deep relationships, which truly foster our soul's growth. Some relationships we hold dear for the support and joy of their blessings, including teachers who influenced us directly or authors, lecturers, and workshop leaders whose wisdom we have sought out. Other people have taught us wonderful lessons by example—by their simple way of being in the world or by quietly letting us know that we are going to be okay. We also acknowledge those relationships whose lessons may have been purchased with pain but that have spurred us in a variety of ways to deepen our soul's wisdom.

Some of our life's teachers support us, whereas others challenge us. Some of our most important lessons are the ones that we like the least. How many teenagers or young adults learn about the cruelty of gossip because the victim of their cruelty is suddenly discovered to be standing within earshot? Sometimes the oppressive, overbearing parent bestows a wonderful gift on the child by instilling the rebellious desire to be a free spirit, who creates life on his or her own terms. We can bless all these people for what they quicken in our own soul's growth.

We also want to bless the friends who stimulate our highest visions and dreams, the ones who remind us who we really are, who see us and love us beyond our current crisis or snit. They remind us of what we are capable. They challenge us when we get off track. They know our darkest secrets and love us anyway. In a world where many of us move frequently and live in a variety of places, friends like these become our extended families.

The first movement in The Magic of Relationships contrasts the times when we feel contracted, internal, and self-reflective with those times when we are able to be expansive, outer-directed, assertive, and capable of extending ourselves to others. It honors those deep friendships that help us move with grace through the swells of this dichotomy. The next moving prayer explores and celebrates the healing warmth of soul friendships. "This is magic, this is love."

The movement helps us fully experience the balance that must be struck between internal nurturing of the spirit and the ability to expand out of ourselves, in order to connect with others and, in turn, to the full experience of life. At different times in our lives, we will find ourselves out of balance on this continuum in one direction or the other—perhaps at times isolating ourselves or at other times taking on the needs and schedules of others to our own detriment. Moving in this pattern highlights where we are and reminds us that sometimes we need to give ourselves more opportunity for self-reflection, whereas at other times we need to "get over ourselves" and get moving out into the world and become more connected and alive.

~

INTENTION: *I walk in balance, accepting my own counsel and receiving the gifts of relationship.*
MUSIC: *"Magic," by Nan Collie, from the CD* Precious Stone, *recorded by Motherlode Music, or other rhythmic New Age music or light jazz.*
EXERCISE: *Aerobic.*

The Magic of Relationships starts with very simple footwork. Begin in a neutral position, feet hip-width apart. Place your right foot behind your left, then open the foot out to the right again. With the step behind, the torso is contracted, and the hands are brought into closed fists crossed at the chest. This brings your physical and emotional awareness inside you. With the step opening out to the side, your hands, arms, and whole body open up and extend to the world. Openness, aliveness, connection, and fullness are the intention of this posture.

To add more interest to the movement, add a cha-cha between sides. Left behind, then left, right, left. Right behind, then right, left, right. Later you can also add a knee lift to the contracted part of the movement. This lends another element of folding inside yourself. Repeat the pattern twenty to sixty times, or for about three to four minutes' worth of music. When you come to completion with this movement, hold in stillness briefly, appreciating the relationships in your life.

Here are the lyrics that inspired this movement. See whether they help you relate to the dance.

### "MAGIC"

This is the fire that's burning on some long cold winter night
This is the light returning when I'm weary of the fight
This is the soul that's singing with the moonlit starry sky
Oh-oh this is magic, this is love.

This is the heart that sought out shelter from the heavy rains
This is the one who stood there naked till the sunlight came
These are the hands that touch the living truth that comes with pain
Oh-oh this is healing, this is love.

This is the woman reaching out now to her brother's/lover's heart
She calls across the canyons, echoes answer in the dark
A common song, a common ground, illusions far apart
Oh-oh this is family, this is love.

—NAN COLLIE

### PERSONAL EXPLORATION

In silence, take your body slowly through the preceding movement and pay attention to which end of the movement feels easier. Is it the folding inside or the thrusting out toward the world? Does the expanded movement make you feel vulnerable? Or does it feel like your natural energy? Do you have so little time for yourself that folding inside feels unnatural? Exploring this theme slowly can help you identify places in which your life can be veering off balance.

# OPEN UP YOUR HEART

Open Up Your Heart exposes the closed places in our hearts that prevent us from creating peace in our own life and in our world. It challenges us to reflect on our life and to choose from this moment forward to act in accord with our heart's true promptings. This dance helps open a pathway from your inner to your outer world, so that you can begin to see the connection between your individual actions and their importance in the greater Universe.

The initial movement encourages you to open your heart physically with a gesture of the hands and to think of where you would like to send a blessing or prayer of intention today. The blessing is sent with an African-based gesture using the torso and a hand wave.

~

INTENTION: *I open my heart and send this blessing to _____ .*
MUSIC: *"Open Up Your Heart," by Suzee Waters Benjamin, from the* CD The Waters Edge, *or rhythmic New Age, Native American–inspired music with defined drumbeats, or soft jazz.*
EXERCISE: *Aerobic.*

Let's begin with a mambo step. Stand in neutral position. Step front and back with your right foot while circling your hands horizontally in front of your chest, palms up. Step to the side with the right foot as you turn your body to the left. This turn leaves your right foot extended behind you in a slight lunge position. As your body faces to the side, send a blessing through the palms of the hands with the wave of the upper torso. The wave is a ripple of the upper spine and rib cage (a chest wave). It begins by lifting the chest as if it were being pulled by a string, then dropping the string, which allows your chest and upper back to sink forward. The torso (or chest) wave is often considered an inherently African gesture. It is almost impossible to do it without feeling the entire chest, rib cage, and heart opening. Repeat the torso wave two times and return to starting position.

Repeat the entire sequence beginning with your left foot and turning to the right on the torso wave. Continue to repeat the dance, alternating sides, twenty to fifty times. Continue to send your blessing until the music comes to a natural end or your mind-body feels complete with the exercise. Repeat your intention once more: "I open my heart and send this blessing to _____."

Optional addition to the dance: When you have become comfortable with the step, you can add a cha-cha between sides. When your right foot is back in lunge, step right, left, right to bring you back to center. Left foot back in lunge, then left, right, left. The cha-cha is optional. Some people find that it adds a feeling of letting go to the mantra.

Here are the lyrics that inspired this dance:

"OPEN UP YOUR HEART"

Open up your heart, Open up your heart
Millions of people are living on the edge
Watching their dreams die, hearing lies and more lies
Are these the final days the prophets have pronounced
Or is there still time to turn this world around

Open up your heart, Open up your heart

We've got a history of hate, a history of war,
Separation, segregation, bigotry, and more
Tradition holds on tight, we fight and fight and fight
But how can we keep score when love's the only door

Open up your heart, Open up your heart

Is nothing innocent or sacred anymore
Do we kill the fatted calf just to see the gore
Do we help the homeless or ship them shore to shore
The fact that we are one cannot be ignored

Open up your heart, Open up your heart

We are all members of the rainbow tribe
Brothers of the sun, sisters of the light
Our mother is the earth, our father is the sky
Let us dance together, it's time that we unite

Open up your heart, Open up your heart
—SUZEE WATERS BENJAMIN

### PERSONAL EXPLORATION

See whether you can create another movement to signify the opening of your heart—one that is personal to your own way of expressing yourself. If movement were the only way to send your blessing to the world, how would your body express that blessing this day?

# FINDING THE HERO WITHIN US

Finding the Hero within Us is a prayerful dance that helps us look inward and conjure up the energy of our innate, archetypal hero. This means discovering the inner strength to find your own voice, speak your own truth, and live it fully, assertively, and passionately. This moving mantra helps us to move beyond our timid introspection and fears of failure. The lyrics that accompany it remind us that we can behave with strength and courage when we live from our spiritual center. The song that inspired this dance, which follows, reminds us that all change comes from the personal courage and commitment of the individual. That's you and me. We have it inside us to create life anew. We are not "just little ol' me" but powerful expressions of spiritual energy.

This dance reminds us of our place in the legion of heroes who are bringing new light and new vision to a world very much in need of healing. Take your place among them!

~

INTENTION: *I take my place among heroes when I speak and act from my highest truth. I act as a hero in my world when I* _____.
MUSIC: *"Hero," by Kathleen Fallon, from the* CD Precious Stone, *recorded by Motherlode Music, or rhythmic, high-energy music.*
EXERCISE: *Aerobic.*

This body prayer is directly connected to the chorus in the song that follows: "There's a hero deep in your heart. Speak your truth and you'll be one." The dance focuses largely on the hand gestures to embody the prayer. It begins with an old-fashioned boxer's victory handclasp, shaking four times to the right of the head, then to the left. Repeat on both sides. Your clasped hands end at your heart, where the hero dwells. The gesture then moves into one of speaking the personal truth of your heart as the hands open out gracefully from your mouth. Continue to extend your hands upward, opening your arms, chest out-

ward to embrace the essence of that truth. The feet step front and back or simply step in place. Repeat this dance thirty to sixty times, depending on your aerobic comfort level. Complete your movements by slowly bringing your hands back to your sides while continuing to step in place for a moment or two.

"HERO"

*Chorus:* There's a hero deep in your heart
Speak your truth and you'll be one.
There's a dream that's waiting to start
Climb that mountain, you'll see one.

Standing on the precipice of what might be
Are you waiting for a miracle to set you free?
Ask for the truth 'cause I've heard it told
That a door will be opened, and the dreamers will come home.
Slow it down, listen hard
Open up, then play your cards.

*Chorus*

Listening to thunder beneath the trees
Do you put yourself in danger so you can see
Lightning shine through raindrops like angel tears?
Riding on the rainbow, just past your fears

Trust your hunch, read the signs.
Look both ways, then cross those lines.

*Chorus*

—KATHLEEN FALLON

### PERSONAL EXPLORATION

Ask yourself whether you can remember a time when you might have responded to a situation with more courage and assertiveness. Then choose your favorite hero or heroine, real or fictional, and imagine how that person might have handled the same situation. Mentally step into his or her shoes and watch yourself relive that situation with your hero or heroine's added strength and courage. Know that this gift of courage is now yours to use.

Now think of a current situation in which you're asked to be courageous. Use the courage gathered from the preceding exploration and add it to the movement described for Finding the Hero within Us (or make up another movement or gesture of your own). Gather the spiritual energy required to facilitate the fulfillment of your need. Have fun with it. Be a superhero! Nobody is watching. Play and learn serious lessons as children do.

# EMPTY BOWL

The theme for this dance was inspired by a song by Suzee Waters Benjamin and challenges us to make use of the hero within. It moves us to use the strength of the hero to bring Spirit into action in our life.

An interesting set of circumstances developed as this dancing prayer series was being planned. First, I found this wonderful piece of music entitled "Empty Bowl," the lyrics of which appear later in this section. The message that we were meant to put Spirit into action as a personal heroic act was readily apparent from the beginning. This idea made me reflect on where I personally wanted to place some commitment in the world. I called the songwriter, Suzee Waters Benjamin, who told me that she had written the song to benefit the Empty Bowl Project, which was started by two teachers in Michigan, Lisa Blackburn and John Hartom, as a community-based fund-raising project to combat hunger in their own hometown.

The project began in the early 1980s when Lisa and John asked the kids in the local high school art department to make a bunch of small ceramic bowls.

Then they persuaded local businesses to donate food for a fund-raising lunch or dinner. They provided entertainment and invited everyone they could think of. Each place setting included one of the bowls made by the high school students. The "Empty Bowl" music accompanied a talk and a slide show of homeless children. The Empty Bowl Foundation makes these same slides available for Empty Bowl fund-raising events throughout the world.

At the end of the talk, people are asked to make a contribution. They are also asked to take the empty bowl home with them and place it somewhere in their cupboard as a reminder of all the bowls in the world that still go empty every day. The best part of the program is that 100 percent of the money goes to the charity chosen by the local sponsoring organization, except for a small voluntary contribution, which the local group sends to the Empty Bowl Foundation. The people who put this program in place truly act from the heart. The funds raised are not depleted by administrative costs and salaries.

My own participation in the Empty Bowl Foundation includes sending the foundation a percentage of the profits from each *Native Spirit* video sold. The Empty Bowl Project has grown to include all fifty states and many countries. The beauty of the system is that it empowers individuals to make a difference in their own communities.

~

INTENTION: *I am willing to act. I am willing to* _____. *(Let your body lead you to the action that is appropriate for you.)*
MUSIC: *"Empty Bowl," by Suzee Waters Benjamin, from the CD* The Waters Edge, *or any rhythmic music.*
EXERCISE: *Aerobic.*

The movements in this dance place the nurturing and succor that a woman's body provides in a prayer of petition to heal the hungry. The first part of the gesture is that of a dancer "receiving bread from the heavens," a kind of spiritual manna. Extend your right hand above your head and imagine that you are pulling bread (sustenance) from the sky to share with people who are in need. The footwork is a simple step front and back with the same foot, a mambo step. This is followed by a hula hip sway. Here the hands fan outward, palms up around the hips, exaggerating the "pelvic bowl." The gesture and movement around the pelvic bowl invite the prayer of petition to fill up the empty bowls of hungry children around the world. The dancer's body becomes the metaphor for the bowl that needs filling. This is a very intimate gesture for

women. Physically expressing the pelvic bowl connects with the personal nurturing our bodies provide to our own children. This prayer to feed the children touches us in very personal and visceral ways. Repeat this movement on alternating sides.

We then add an African gesture of women's nourishment. The hands are held palm up under the breasts, as you wave your chest and upper back as you did in the Open Up Your Heart dance. This movement suggests a nursing mother opening her pulsating heart and her body. Reflect on an area in your

life in which you are willing to extend yourself into the larger world community. Matthew Fox calls this the *via transformativa*. In India this is the path of dharma, the path of service, experiencing our soul's connection to the rest of the world.

Complete this prayer with the natural end of the music or when you feel complete with the exercise. Remember the right action that you are willing to bring into your day.

## "EMPTY BOWL"

He was born in a cradle of sorrow
With nothing to do but cry
He would cry for his supper
Cry for his loving, cry for his lullabies

Mama she'd come and rock him
And wipe the tears from his eyes
She would try and console him
Kiss him and hold him
But he was not satisfied

*Chorus:* Have mercy, have mercy on this hungry child
Have mercy, have mercy on his soul
Tell me, why do some have so much
While others don't have enough
Put the bread of life into his empty bowl
Put the bread of life into his empty bowl

Now are we so blind that we cannot see
This poverty belongs to you and me.
The ocean and the air we breathe
Connects us for eternity
We are one family.

We've got silos of grain, we've got fortune and fame,
We've got pedigreed cat food in a crystal vase.
And the cost of all this glamour
Could attempt to feed the famine
If we'd open up our hearts to the human race

*Chorus*

Now corruption and greed have cast their spell
And the ravages of war we know too well
But history will agree that only time can tell
Will we make this place a heaven or a hell
Will we make this place a heaven or a hell

*Chorus*

—SUZEE WATERS BENJAMIN

## PERSONAL EXPLORATION

Emptiness can be experienced in mind, body, or spirit. Hold an empty kitchen bowl in your hands. Slowly circulate it in front of you in a spiral motion. Begin at the lower abdomen. Continue the spiraling motion and gradually raise the bowl up overhead. Keep in mind all the ways that your bowl (your life) is full. Express your gratitude for this fullness. With bowl overhead, you might pause for a few seconds to "pay intention" to the air you take in and consider how a simple thing like air nourishes the body. Then slowly begin a descending spiral with the bowl, asking yourself what gifts of the mind, body, and spirit you might offer the world from your own fullness. End the exercise by holding the bowl low on your abdomen, allowing the wisdom of your body to speak to you about receiving and sharing.

# BLESSING OF THE ANCESTORS

This dance was inspired by a Native American blessing song recorded by Motherlode Music. It is the final aerobic sequence in the chapter. I like to use it as a comforting self-blessing and to acknowledge with gratitude the energy of the embodied prayers I've just completed. The words below are a personal blessing to you.

~

INTENTION: *When my life is done, I will have left something good on the earth.*
MUSIC: *"Blessing," by Mike Brewer and Tom Shipley, from the CD* Precious Stone, *recorded by Motherlode Music; Native American flute music that includes a defined rhythm; or other flowing, rhythmic music of your choice.*
EXERCISE: *Aerobic.*

The first steps embrace the bodily attitude of childlike acceptance of the blessing. Begin with four light and lyrical skips to the front and four skips back, allowing the arms and hands to lightly and joyfully swing side to side.

The next step and gesture suggest receiving this blessing from the realms of the Great Spirit and spreading it around us out to the world. The gesture receives the blessing with arms open and spreads it out with palms down, as if

spreading it on the earth. This expresses the intention "May I leave something good behind." The footwork is a box step: right foot crosses in front, left crosses in front, right steps back, left steps back. If this seems too complicated, simply step four counts in place. Let the footwork remind you that you are connected to the earth. Continue the movement until the natural end of the music or until you feel that your body has had enough. Bring your feet together and hold the hand gesture of blessing the earth for another moment. Repeat your intention for the day: "I will leave something good behind today."

Here is the blessing that generated this dance:

### "BLESSING"

Should your blankets be torn, may your breezes blow warm.
May your treasures be what you find.
May the burdens you bear like your bounty be shared.
May you leave something good behind.
Would the sky and the land rise to your command,
May your senses cut like the knife.
Live in peace with the earth in death as in birth.
May you prosper and lead a good life.
                                        —MIKE BREWER AND TOM SHIPLEY

### PERSONAL EXPLORATION

Imagine what other bodily postures or gestures could signify receiving a great prize or present. If you get stuck, think of a five-year-old at his or her birthday party. If you had the abilities of a great wizard to share all of your gifts with the world, what would that sharing gesture look like?

# BLESSING THE DIVINE WOMB

Blessing the Divine Womb uses imagery of the Divine Mother. The beautifully written song by Colleen Fulmer that follows presents the world as a sacred womb or sanctuary of love and grace. We are asked to revere and bless the earth and remember that it is all sacred space. The poetic lyrics encourage a mind-set of profound gratitude for the blessings of this earth.

In this dance we mimic the movements of the Great Mother. This is a very powerful energy for women. Imagining the Great Mystery in a female form, we begin to recognize an energy that is magnetic and pregnant with possibilities. We might imagine we hear Her singing our name into existence, combing our hair one last time before sending us off to our birth. She has mothered us all. She has nurtured us with Her wisdom, strength, and great love. Women know this in our bodies as well as in our minds. This dance helps us to remember.

~

INTENTION: *All Creation is sacred. I walk in gratitude for Her gifts.*
MUSIC: *"Blessing the Divine Womb," by Colleen Fulmer, from the CD Dancing Sophia's Circle, or any soft, flowing, rhythmic music of your choice.*
EXERCISE: *Cooldown.*

Begin facing to your right and take four walking steps in that direction, beginning with your left foot. Then turn. Repeat to your left. Palms face toward the earth at hip level. Your palms sense the energy of the holy ground and send a blessing to her. Repeat fifteen to twenty times.

The next movement mimics the loving embrace of the Divine Mother for

Her beloved children. With feet shoulder-width apart, step to the side with your right foot into a squatting position. Your hands and arms circle around your pelvis, or the sacred womb, then reach around the front and gather to the heart. The physical metaphor is of the Great Mother giving birth and reaching around to embrace Her children, caring for them, and gathering them ever so lovingly to Her. Repeat this sequence four to ten times. Come to completion by bringing your feet together and taking several deep breaths. Listen to the words that gave birth to the dance.

## "BLESSING THE DIVINE WOMB"

O Sacred Womb of love and grace
We can feel you all around us
We lift our hands to touch and bless you
For we are held and carried in this holy place.

Blessed be this womb
Where we can move, and dance and dream
Blessed be this womb
That holds us safe and warm within.

Blessed be this womb,
Where Mama's heart is beating strong
Blessed be this womb
She rocks us gently to her songs.

Blessed be this womb
Your wondrous love encircles us
Blessed be this womb
Where darkness folds and nurtures us.

—COLLEEN FULMER

### PERSONAL EXPLORATION

This next body prayer can be done at any time by men or women. Women who are menopausal often find it even more powerful. Because they will not be carrying another life, they feel freer exploring the inner planes of creative possibilities.

Begin with hands folded over the lower abdomen, over your womb. Men can use the same hand placement or hold their hands over their genitals. Breathe and bring your awareness into this part of your body. Know it to be the center of your own creativity. Experience yourself as pregnant with possibility. What is it that your life is birthing today? What possibilities would you like to bring forth? What seeds of wisdom are you creating for future generations?

The birthing part of this movement is an improvisation. Allow yourself to move in a way that expresses the birthing process to you. Be as calm or as wild as you see fit. Feel the passion and power of the Creative Mother moving energy through your body. Give birth to yourself. Give birth to your highest and brightest dreams, affirmations for today and hopes for tomorrow. I like to do this movement to earthy, rhythmic African drumming. Dance and give birth to yourself!

# SOPHIA

We end this series of dances with stretches. There are rich visual and musical symbols in the poetry that follows. The words are praise for *Sophia*, an ancient feminine term for "wisdom." Many indigenous cultures make spiritual associations with the four directions, and this song calls on the wisdom of the directions, one by one. They are most often associated with the four elements of air, earth, fire, and water.

The wisdom of the east is associated with air, symbolized here by the feather. This imagery speaks of spiritual guidance, the "whispering of Spirit" in our ears, the messages from the ancestors telling us what to do, and all manner of Divine inspiration.

The wisdom of the south is associated with fire, symbolized here by the candle. The fire represents the qualities of warmth, passion, courage, strength of will and purpose, and the fire of Spirit in our lives.

The wisdom of the west is associated with water, represented by a pitcher of flowing water. Water represents emotional flexibility and the ability to change and flow with the needs of the current moment. It can change forms from liquid to solid to gas to fit its environment, thus representing change and spiritual transformation.

The wisdom of the north is associated with the earth, symbolized by ground corn being scattered on the earth. In the tradition of the four elements, the earth represents many things—the grounding of Spirit in matter, completion and fruition, care and nurturing, the strength of the mountain, the strength of our beingness.

~

INTENTION: *These are my nature: air, fire, water, and earth. Breath, radiance, feelings, and grounded roots.*
MUSIC: *"Epiclesis," by Colleen Fulmer, from the CD* Dancing Sophia's Circle, *or any relaxing, free-flowing instrumental music.*
EXERCISE: *Stretches.*

These images feed us as we relax into our stretching and prepare for the time of musical meditation. The first stretch begins on your back. Bring your knee to your chest, holding your leg underneath the knee to support it. This stretches the hip, buttock, and hamstring (back of the thigh). The second stretch is the bent-knee stretch. Holding behind your left thigh, straighten out your leg until you feel a stretch behind the thigh. Hold. Do not pull hard. Next, press the thigh into your hands, letting the hands resist the pressure of the thigh. Hold for a count of five and release. Pull and repeat the bent-knee stretch, and you will probably find that you have gained a bit more flexibility. This is called antagonistic stretching. It begins with a stretch, then a contraction, followed by another stretch.

Now roll on your left side, so that you can stretch the front of the thigh. Holding on to your ankle, keeping both knees close to the floor, pull back on your right leg, stretching the front of the thigh. If this is difficult for you, try a towel, as illustrated in the photo. Turn on your back again and repeat the same series of stretches on the other leg.

Next, roll on your side, bringing the knees up almost to a fetal position. Place your hands behind your head with your elbows in front of your face. Take a breath in and exhale, opening and gently twisting the upper back. Let your eyes follow the upper elbow. Stay here for about twenty seconds, breathing deeply. Then lift the top leg, followed by your other leg, and repeat the twist on your side. Come to completion by rolling onto your back or side and resting for as long as you'd like.

Here is the poetry of the four directions:

### "EPICLESIS"

O Wisdom of the East O Wisdom of the East
Sophia, Sophia
Come breathe in us Come breathe in us,
Sophia, Sophia

O Wisdom of the South O Wisdom of the South
Sophia, Sophia
Come shine in us Come shine in us
Sophia, Sophia

O Wisdom of the West O Wisdom of the West
Sophia, Sophia
Come flow through us Come flow through us
Sophia, Sophia

O Wisdom of the North O Wisdom of the North

Sophia, Sophia
Come root in us Come root in us
Sophia, Sophia!

—COLLEEN FULMER

# THE WATERS EDGE

I like to complete a dancing series by relaxing into a private time of meditation or by listening to a piece of music with or without lyrics. I try to imagine that the music is washing over and through me as I lie or sit comfortably.

The poetry that follows is from one of my all-time favorite pieces of music for meditation. It has a Native American sensibility, reverential and deeply moving. Some people tape-record the words of songs they like, so they can hear them as a spoken prayer during meditation.

~

MUSIC: *"The Waters Edge," by Suzee Waters Benjamin, from the CD of the same name, or any other soft meditational music, especially Native American flute music.*
EXERCISE: *Relaxation/meditation.*

To begin, simply find a comfortable position in which to relax deeply, so the words of the meditation may take their full effect in your awareness.

## "THE WATERS EDGE"

Great Spirit above and below us,
Your power is everything we see.
Great Spirit around and within us,
Your love is everything that breathes.

May our hearts be as light as the winged ones,
Our trust as strong as the stones,
Our vision as vast as the ocean,
Our truth as bright as the sun.

For all these blessings we give thanks.
Teach us the sacred and the true.
Help us to find our way back home
Into our hearts with you.
Into our hearts with you.

Come to the waters edge,
Where the land meets the sea.
Come to the waters edge,
And dream with me.

—SUZEE WATERS BENJAMIN

# Chapter 7

# DANCING A MIRACLE: BANISHING FEAR AND REACHING FOR THE MIRACLE OF LOVE

The two dominant themes for this set of prayers are: love is our natural essence, and fear is the opposite of love. From love naturally come all other positive attributes, such as compassion, patience, and integrity. These dances are meant to foster your growth as a loving person and help you see the places in which you act out of fear, so that you can bring love to those situations or feelings. Miracles can occur when we look fearlessly at our negative thinking and behaviors and choose to change in order to act in accordance with Spirit. Just as you create concentric circles when you toss a pebble into a lake, you create ever-extending, increasing goodness when you act from love.

Next time you're in an argument with someone you care about, see whether you can act out of love by deciding that being right is less important than being loving. This internal miracle alone can create peace in the world.

These prayerful dances give you the opportunity to examine and commit to a path of the greatest miracles of all—love and peace.

## IN THE NAME OF LOVE

When beginning a series of dancing prayers, I always warm up the body with slow, easy movement. I like to establish a specific intention to hold on to. With this movement, hold the intention of acting in the name of love. No matter what our life circumstances are today, we can decide to rise above the dualism of "good and bad" by acting in the name of love. We are reminded that as we let go of the judgments of the life around us, we are free to act from our soul's higher purpose. We can open to love and pass it on to the world around us. We thus become spiritual alchemists who bring golden light to a world in need of healing. Acting in the name of love is a statement of intention for the way in which we would like to live our lives. It's a wonderful affirmation to hold as you open your body to movement and set your mission statement for the rest of your day.

INTENTION: *Today I will act in the name of love.*
MUSIC: *"Real Love," by Donna Marie Cary, from the tape of the same name, or any soft, free-flowing music.*
EXERCISE: *Warm-up.*

The movements used during this piece are done in a free-flowing fashion that allows you to be open to this affirmation.

Begin standing with feet hip-width apart, arms hanging comfortably at your sides. Slowly create "soft knees" and reach overhead with three winged arm reaches, using the movement to open mind, body, and spirit. Starting in neutral position, reach your arms out and up in an arc at the sides of your body

until the backs of your hands touch above your head. Then bring your arms out to your sides around shoulder level, palms up. These overhead reaches are about making a connection with the higher self and the Holy Source. If these movements connect you to something else, by all means go with your own feelings. Reaching up is an almost universal gesture that symbolizes reaching to that which is greater than ourselves.

The next movement mimics big bird wings, which symbolize freedom in body and spirit. This is the same movement you just did, except that the backs of your hands meet out in front of your torso and then open to the sides with palms up. Just relax and let your body take you to the spirit of freedom.

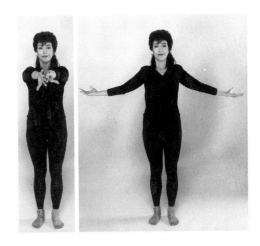

The next set begins with eight shoulder rolls on one side. Next, see whether you can roll your hip in a circle on the same side. This loosens the shoulder, upper back, chest, hip, and lower back. Now let your elbow lead the shoulder roll, which makes the movement even bigger, and finally let the whole arm get into the circular motion. Try to maintain the hip roll at the same time. This is a wonderful way of relaxing and loosening up the entire spine as well as the arms and shoulders. Play with the idea of letting the different areas lead the movement and you will be able to explore the ways in which the body is connected, with all the different parts moving together. Then repeat the entire sequence on the other side of the body.

The above series of movements stretches and prepares the legs. Face the left, placing your right calf behind you with your heel on the floor to stretch the calf. Bring your arms up and out at shoulder level with your palms up. From this position bend the front knee to stretch the front of the left hip. Bring your hands to prayer position over your head. Then place your hands on your front thigh, bend the back knee, straighten the front knee, and flatten your lower back to stretch the back of your thigh (hamstrings). Repeat this series on the other side as well. Hold all stretches for six to ten seconds.

A series of lower-back releases warms up this area as well. Do these by facing front and placing your hands on the front of your thighs to support your weight. Press the lower back up and then release it down, moving back and forth eight to ten times.

The warm-up ends with winged arms opening again one last time "in the name of love."

## PERSONAL EXPLORATION

Whenever warming up the body, check in with yourself to see what parts of yourself need attention before entering into more vigorous movement. Take a kind of physical/emotional inventory and pay attention to what your body reveals. As you admit your body into your spiritual practice more often, its wisdom will become more apparent to you. Perhaps your ankle will need more stretching one day or your calves on another day after a hike you took the day before. The body will communicate its needs more clearly as you learn to appreciate and include it as a magnificent vehicle for spiritual expression.

# FROM THE HEART

The gestures in this next movement series relate directly to the words in the chorus of the song "From the Heart": "Let me feel what is real. Let me heal what is not. Let me live every moment coming straight from the heart."

It is very easy in our high-tech world to keep ourselves distracted from the full emotional impact of our environment. There are a thousand avenues that can numb our senses and prevent us from being present in our lives: TV, music, E-mail, the Internet, telephones, magazines, newspapers, drugs, and alcohol, to name a few. The gestures in this dance affirm our commitment to being awake and mindful to what is going on in our lives. It is a powerful call not only to experience fully the people and events of our lives but also to reflect deeply on our feelings about them without being distracted from our truth.

INTENTION: *I will live my life authentically with the fullness of my heart.*

MUSIC: *"From the Heart," by Scott Kalechstein, from the CD* Eyes of God, *or other rhythmic New Age, soft jazz, or light rock music.*

EXERCISE: *Aerobic.*

The above footwork, a mambo step, is repeated during the entire dance. Starting in neutral position, step front with your right foot, then step back with the same foot and return to neutral. Switch feet and repeat the step on your left side. As always, the feet are the least important element of this body prayer. You may choose simply to step in place or not to move at all, using only the arm gestures. On the phrase "Let me feel what is real," reach one arm at a time overhead to call the fullness of life's experiences into your heart area.

The next gesture expresses "Let me heal what is not." This gesture mimics the hands in a healing act. Think of massaging someone or the laying on of hands. With this movement, we can imagine a person, a situation, or even the earth receiving the healing of our intentions and actions. We become facilitators of a healing, evolving planet. Your hands make two circles with palms down at waist level.

The next gesture is a large movement, which embraces the enormity of our lives and their inherent importance when fully lived with spiritual power and intention. We are spiritual warriors making bold contributions to planetary growth. Allow this largesse to speak with this movement. Make two large arm circles overhead, accompanying the phrase "Let me live every moment." Because this is a large movement that opens the chest and stretches the torso as well as the arms, you can really get the feeling of being fully alive.

The final gesture reflects the phrase "coming straight from the heart." Once more we acknowledge that the supply of love in our lives cannot be depleted. It is endless and eternal, as it wells forth from an infinite Source. This is the truest picture of your radiant essence. The gesture provides an "Amen" to this powerful and beautiful affirmation. Make two circles with the hands at the level of your heart. The palms are up and open, drawing energy from the core of the heart and sending it out into the world. I will repeat this dance for three to five minutes' worth of music. Continue this until the natural end of your music or until your body signals you to stop. Bring your feet back to neutral and hold for a moment with your hands over your heart. Repeat the affirmation to act from your heart.

Here are the full lyrics of the song that inspired the dance:

### "FROM THE HEART"

*Chorus:* Let me feel what is real
Let me heal what is not
Let me live every moment
Coming straight from the heart.

All I really want is an open heart
All I really need is an open heart
I have an endless supply of love in my heart.

A child's faith is all I need
To live every moment
Coming straight from the love in my heart.

*Chorus*

—SCOTT KALECHSTEIN

### PERSONAL EXPLORATION

In a quiet moment, create other gestures that are true for you to express the phrases of this song. As you employ these gestures, consider places in your life that are less than authentic expressions of who you are and what you would like to have for yourself. What do you really feel about your job, your marriage, your spiritual practice, and your relationships with specific friends and loved ones?

In what ways can you change those things that you would like to be different? How would you bring change, healing, or a higher order of relating to these areas? What are you willing to do to create your life in the image of your beliefs and values? This need not require huge upheavals. Small, incisive, persistent corrections each day can change the patterns of our habitual thoughts, behaviors, and personal reactions. For most of us, it is in the small details of life that our awareness can gain the most growth. What are the ways you could change to most clearly reflect the way you would live if you were always able to come from the heart—the heart of truth as well as the heart of love?

# NO LIMIT

This prayerful movement was inspired by a song written as a statement of the affirmation "There's no limit to what I can do." It seeks to bring our attention to the places where we hold limited thinking, replacing them with the idea of infinite possibilities.

First, form a clear image of your dream(s) that you will retain throughout the sequence of movements. When dancing this dance, feed your dreams with your energy, your breath, and your positive intention, as if you were sending the energy of Creation out from your fingertips, turning possibility into reality. Remember the exercise you did in chapter 1 on focused intention.

Sometimes it's difficult to know what we want in life and to believe we are worthy of receiving it. It's important to activate and expand our personal vision of our possibilities. We need to do this before we can decide what actions are required to turn a dream into reality. Use this dance to expand the horizons of your possibilities.

Take a few moments in stillness, breathing three deep, cleansing breaths. Allow the vision of your highest dream to surface. Hold this image in mind as you affirm the intention that goes with this dance.

~

INTENTION: *I believe that my highest dreams are possible and that they are becoming manifest.*
MUSIC: *"No Limit," by Donna Marie Cary, from the CD* Real Love, *or other rhythmic New Age, soft jazz, or Native American music.*
EXERCISE: *Aerobic.*

Stand up in a wide, relaxed stance, with your knees bent in a squatting position. Reach your right arm up and across your body to the left and then back to neutral. Then reach your left arm up and across to the right side. Continue alternate reaches with your palms down. The feet flare slightly out. As you reach across your body with your right hand, pivot on the toes of your right foot, so that your knees are both pointing in the same direction as you reach. Repeat this movement for twenty to fifty repetitions, or less if your body tires with fewer repetitions.

Let your eyes follow your hands, adding intention to the movement. In this case, you are reaching to the far horizons of your dreams. Reach and extend your body and mind to the highest possibilities and aspirations of your

soul. What are they? Breathe and dance power into them. Your dreams are coming true.

The second step comes from a Native American dance. It represents the flight of the eagle. Allow yourself to feel the freedom of the soaring eagle in this step. Let your imagination soar and your dreams expand with the freedom of flying. The break step begins with extending your arms out to the sides, your right hand pointing above your head and left hand below like the wings of a flying eagle. Step twice in place with your left foot. Then reverse hand positions and step twice on the other side. When you get a rhythm going back and forth between sides, your arms really begin to feel the flight of the eagle soaring.

The last part of the dance repeats the first step, only now reach with palms

up, as if you have something to give away and send to the farthest reaches of the world. This gesture acknowledges the profound gifts living inside you that you are willing to share with the remotest recesses of humanity. Let all the light you carry travel to the far horizons. It is your gift and a deep prayer to share the light of your soul with the rest of the world. Come to completion at the natural end of the music or when your body is ready for a breather. After a few moments of stillness, take a deep breath and reaffirm, "My dreams are coming into form now."

PERSONAL EXPLORATION

One of the boldest and bravest statements of demanding new possibilities comes in the process of moving through the birth canal to take our new birth. Quietly meditate and imagine that you are sitting comfortably in your mother's womb. Now allow yourself to feel longing for something more. Notice that the softness and warmth around you continue. Listen to the pleasant, reassuring rhythm of your mother's heartbeat. And yet something in you stirs and calls to you, and every part of you knows that you must move toward this calling.

As you sit in the current comfortable womb of your life today, what is it that calls you farther now? Is there something just out of clear awareness calling to you? Is there something holding you back from reaching toward it? A dream almost too sweet to consider?

A brightness that exists as an idea just beyond your awareness captures your attention. Ah! I want to live! I want to be born! You move now into the birth canal, which is not at all comfortable. It's tight and suffocating, yet you bravely push on into the idea of light just beyond your full comprehension. What is it you need to move through today to reach fully for your long-held dream?

Finally you break through into the light of a new life! You draw your first breath! Ahhh! Spirit has sung you into being. Spirit has breathed through you—and is breathing still. If you listen in the stillness, you can still hear Spirit singing the dream of your life. Each breath is a part of the song. Allow yourself the gift of exploring the Spirit song of your life.

# HANDLE YOURSELF WITH CARE

This song reminds us that we are loved. We are precious in the eyes of Spirit, which also sees us as innocent in our hearts. This is sometimes hard for people to accept within themselves. Many of us have been harshly criticized and told that we don't measure up. Some of us have been raised to believe that we are guilty of "original sin." This leaves many with a sense of profound unworthiness.

We do have the power to choose another vision of ourselves and those around us—one that tells us we are innocent. In our hearts we are like children, trying our best to unfold our souls within the confines of our earthbound experiences. This is a grand adventure but not an easy one. It takes devotion, courage, wisdom, and love to hold to the vision of our collective innocence.

How does this vision change us and the world? Think of a mother watching her child's first efforts at learning how to walk. The child will fall many times before taking a successful first step. Does she call those first attempts a failure? Does she blame the child for not measuring up to his four-year-old sibling? Does she regard the child's unsuccessful attempts as a sign of some inherent evil? Of course not.

So it is with our efforts at unfolding our spiritual awareness. Although we do not always behave in ways that reveal the higher parts of our nature, and there are times when we get down and dirty, impatient, and judgmental of others or ourselves, we can choose to see these challenges as merely temporary setbacks. They are like the child's momentary fall on her bottom. The important lesson is that we keep ourselves moving. Clear away the thought of failure. Acknowledge that "Yes, I am still human." If we didn't have spiritual work left to do, we probably would not still be here in this earth suit. Make the appropriate correction without judgment and move on. Imagine the Universal Presence of Love, watching each setback and each self-correction with the same vision and appreciation that the mother holds for her child attempting to walk. We are attempting to awaken into Love's vision of us. With courage and perseverance we can leave behind the negative cultural messages of our time and move into a higher vision of love and self-acceptance.

~

INTENTION: *I am loved and accepted.*
MUSIC: *"Handle Yourself with Care," by Scott Kalechstein, from the CD* **Eyes of God**, *or other rhythmic, New Age, soft rock, or light jazz music.*
EXERCISE: *Aerobic.*

Holding the thought of divine acceptance and love in mind, we can move on to the chorus of the song that inspired this dance: "Handle yourself with care, there's a precious child of God in there." The body prayer for this piece goes along with these words.

The footwork, if you wish to use it, forms a pattern of front, back, side, together. Begin standing with feet hip-width apart, arms hanging comfortably at your sides. Take a few moments to inhale and exhale deeply three times, and when you feel centered, begin the movement. Step your right foot forward, then bring it behind its starting position, then step to your right side with the same foot, then back to starting position. Switch and repeat on the other side.

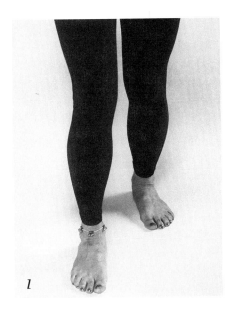

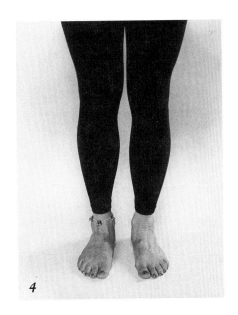

Place both of your hands a few inches from the crown of your head, palms down. Then slowly bring both your hands to the level of your ears with the intention of clearing away negative thoughts, especially those about yourself. This gesture goes with the front and back step. The next gesture goes with the side step. It is a self-hug, acknowledging the "precious child of God" that you are. Stepping to the side while doing the self-hug allows the entire torso to

sway and relax into the acceptance of this hug. Make the spine as loose as it can be, as you feel and accept this statement. Repeat the entire sequence on alternating sides for three to five minutes.

Of all the body prayers in the Aerobic Prayer dances, the self-hug is the one that many of my students find the most difficult. If that's the case for you, think of your feelings as a barometer of your need to repeat this body prayer as often as possible. How can we expect to experience the presence of Divine Love if we have difficulty accepting our own innocence? We *are* worthy, or we would never have been given the gift of incarnation. We were trusted enough to be given the opportunity to experience life on the material plain with all its pitfalls and distractions. Until we truly acknowledge our worthiness and accept ourselves exactly as we are today, we can never truly experience love, and the soul will go on feeling unnourished and alone.

As *A Course in Miracles* tells us, "Choose once again." If you realize that you have made a less-than-perfect choice, make the correction without judgment and choose again.

Here are the words that inspired this dance:

### "HANDLE YOURSELF WITH CARE"

Once I thought by now I'd be Mr. Functionality
Perfect and complete in every way,
But I still get lost and then get found.
As I walk the sacred stumbling ground
I need to reassure me I'm ok.
I'm all grown up the world can see
But that is just one side of me.
I'm also a tender child finding my way,
I sometimes stumble in the dirt,
I have a heart that can be hurt
And so I hear a voice within me say,

*Chorus:* Handle yourself with care,
There's a precious child of God in there.
Handle yourself with care,
There's a precious child of God in there.
Handle yourself with care,
There's a precious child of God in there.

There's a judge inside who's sometimes strong
Convinced I'm doing my whole life wrong,
So quick to rise up to my prosecution
But as I grow it's getting clear
That that is just the voice of fear
And gentleness my only real solution,
For how can the child in me feel safe
If I'm trying to wear myself in chains?
There must be another way to grow.
The petals of my heart open in a loving self-environment
A flower grows and blooms when it's given the room.

*Chorus*

So I live life day to day,
Some obstacles get in my way
And though I grow, I see the strength that birthed.
I still get lost and then get found
As I walk the sacred stumbling ground
Our life is getting sweeter on this earth.
Reaching out make heart connection
Making my peace with imperfection
Finding out the world needs what I have to give.
For as I love the child in me
My heart extends so naturally
I can lend the world my shoulder when my cup is running over.

*Chorus*

—SCOTT KALECHSTEIN

## PERSONAL EXPLORATION

Close your eyes and imagine a time when you reacted to a situation or a person in a way that was less than skillful. Go ahead and let yourself feel whatever emotions come up.

Now allow the gentle presence of Divine Love to take form and stand by you. This presence may take an unfamiliar form. It may show up as a faceless figure, a familiar guide, an energy, or a religious figure such as Jesus, Buddha, or Kuan-Yin. Bring the figure that is right for you into the scene. Watch the scene again, with Divine Love at your side watching it with you. Ask the Presence of

Love to show you how you might have handled the situation in a more skillful fashion.

Notice especially the feelings of compassion for all parties that Divine Love maintains while handling the situation truthfully and skillfully.

Now step inside the shoes and presence of this being and go through the situation with the same qualities yourself. Ask for help if needed. See yourself maintain the same feeling of compassion and understanding for all parties in the interaction. Notice that the qualities of love and understanding do not conflict with appropriate behavioral boundaries.

When you have completed this learning experience, go over it again, this time on your own with the guiding presence there as support. Repeat the exercise until it becomes easy. This is a powerful exercise to train habitual mental pathways into a more evolved proactive set of responses. Repeat the exercise until you feel that the next time a similar circumstance occurs, you could quickly react with the same wisdom and compassion that you have just learned and now know to be the truth of who you are.

Next, begin to walk around the room silently or with music. Invite the embodied Presence of Love once more to join you. Imagine again that you are stepping into Love's shoes and body. Keep walking. Does your posture change as you imagine yourself in the presence of Love? What is your gait like? Hurried or slow? Does your external vision of the world around you change? Continue for several minutes to experience the Presence of Love moving through your body and mind. When you are finished, thank the Presence of Love for teaching and being with you in this way.

## HEALING NIGHTMARES AND NEGATIVE THINKING

This next song promotes the idea of eliminating negative thoughts, especially your fears. Our culture constantly throws at us pictures of violence and tragedy, images of superficial perfection and ideal beauty, and commercial standards of wealth and material success. We fight a discontented sense that we must have more, be more, and do more, and it is important for our emotional health to make a deliberate effort to stop and ask ourselves, "How much is enough?" More important, we must remember to stop and say, "Thank you for all I have," and "Thank you for all I am today."

This next embodied prayer is a vehicle for naming and metaphorically kicking away thoughts that are not serving us well. What recurring thoughts plague your personal world and inhibit your sense of peace? Place them in that spot toward which you're kicking. (This is similar to the exercise in chapter 4, but the intention differs. There you were kicking to coordinate your intention with your will and follow through. Here you will be using your focus to eliminate those thoughts that do not represent the highest truth of who you are and who you are becoming.) This is a wonderful power move. Have fun with it. This exercise gives you a great opportunity to experience yourself as a spiritual warrior. Look at the beauty of your inner strength!

INTENTION: *I am in charge of my thoughts. I release all thoughts that do not reflect the best of me.*
MUSIC: *"Nightmares," by Donna Marie Cary, from the CD* Real Love, *or any defined rhythmic, New Age, African drums, or hard-driving rock music.*
EXERCISE: *Aerobic.*

The footwork starts with a grapevine: Begin traveling to your right side. Your right foot steps to the side. Your left foot crosses behind the right. The right steps to the side again, followed by a tap of the left foot. Then reverse to the other direction.

Once you become comfortable with the step, bring the tap up to a small side kick if you can. Push through the heel. Do not snap or hyperextend the knee on the kick. Choose a spot on the floor or wall with your eyes and kick to that spot. Choose the point, focus, and follow through with the kick. As you kick, exhale and let out a sound. Repeat the steps for twenty to fifty repetitions.

The second step can help you catch your breath. As your hand circles the head during this step, you create the image of clearing away your limited, habitual thinking. Circle your head to capture the unwanted thought, then push it away from you. Banish it from your life. Capture and dispatch whatever is not in alignment with your highest dream: "I'm not smart enough to run my own business." Throw it away! "I'm too fat to have the perfect mate." Throw it away! "I'm not good at handling money. I'll never be comfortable." Throw it away! "Sex can't be spiritual." Throw it away! "I don't have time to have a spiritual practice." Throw it away! Have fun with this part. You know the junky thoughts that rattle around inside. Toss 'em out with vigor. It's fun to clean your mental house. It's an act of spiritual power.

Simply step behind with your right foot and then step to the side. Repeat with the other foot, step behind, and open. As you step behind with your right foot, encircle your head with your right hand and then push away to the side as the foot opens to the side step. Reverse and repeat on the other side. Repeat on alternating sides twenty to fifty times. Come to a close at the natural end of the music or when your body has had enough. This is a high-intensity exercise. As you begin to return to stillness, notice the powerful energy coursing through you as you move with a heightened sense of possibilities.

### PERSONAL EXPLORATION

This next exploration is really a simple technique that I learned from my friend Diane. One day I watched Diane make a move with her hand that looked as if she were swatting away a fly from in front of her face, only it was January, and there are no flies where I live in winter. I asked her, "What are you doing?" She told me that she was banishing a thought that came up that she didn't want to have anymore. What a wonderful prayer! It can be done anywhere, unobtrusively.

We are all susceptible to negative images that work on us in ways we aren't even aware of. What mother hasn't had a pang of some disaster when she puts her young child on a school bus for the first time? What about those of you with new teenage drivers in the house? Where does this junk come from? And what do we do about it?

It is important that we find ways to train the mind in a different direction. Thoughts become magnetic when we dwell on them. Earlier I mentioned the old proverb that goes, "What we think about is sure to come about." That is why we need a tool to help us retrain the uninvited negative thoughts that enter our minds.

To do the banishing prayer, simply pass your hand quickly in front of your eyes as if you were clearing your vision with the back of your hand, like a wiper clearing mist from the windshield of a car. Bring the hand away from your field of vision toward the earth. With the first part of the motion, we clear the negative thought. With the second part, we send the thought back to the fires at the center of the earth for cleansing and transformation. The internal prayer may go something like, "Begone. I cleanse my mind screen." We may not be able to entirely eliminate the negative thoughts that come to us unbidden, but we can break the spell of their power over our thinking. This simple motion is a uniquely powerful vehicle for creating energetic change in our personal lives and for healing the collective mind of our culture.

I have the fantasy that it will sweep across the nation. I would love to drive on a busy urban freeway and see people all around me clearing their vision instead of making the other hand gestures we see all too frequently.

## PEACE IN THE WORLD BEGINS WITH ME

When I use the following movement in retreats and classes, it repeatedly evokes the deep trance state of moving prayer. The main chant is an ancient Sanskrit phrase that poignantly bridges Eastern and Western sensibility. The phrase "Om Namo Bhagavate Vasudevaya" translates as, "Thy will be done on earth as it is in heaven." With this universal acknowledgment of surrender to Divine Order, the stage is set for the deep, self-reflective prayer for peace that follows.

I described this movement in chapter 1, in the section on forgiveness. I like to use it here as a cooldown movement because it fits well into the theme of being a spiritual warrior who does battle with negative, limited thought and who transmutes that energy into the creation of a peaceful mind-set. The words of the song (which appear later in this section) next express, "May the warriors find peace within. Let the healing of the earth begin." In developing the embodied prayer for this phrase, it became obvious that prayer for world (outer) peace is impossible without personal (inner) peace. So the gestures reflect both the interior quest for our own personal peace and the exterior manifestation that naturally follows a peaceful internal state.

~

INTENTION: *I choose peace for myself and for all beings.*
MUSIC: *"Prayer for the Warriors," by Sophia, from the CD* Sophia Returns, *or other free-flowing, rhythmic, evocative, New Age instrumental music.*
EXERCISE: *Cooldown.*

Starting in neutral position, step your right foot front, then back to starting position (one mambo). The hands are in fists, pulsing twice above the head and twice at waist level. The body feeling is one of tension and contraction. Next, step to the side, opening the arms, chest, and entire torso. Allow the whole body to flow and release as fluidly as you can into this open position. Fully release the contraction of the fisted warrior. The feeling in the body is as

if you were taking a great big gulp of fresh air after holding your breath underwater. Some people like to release a big breathy sound, "Ahhhhhhh." Breathe and relax with this part of the movement.

Next, we acknowledge that it is from our heart's own center that peace can be created in the world. From our own sacred heart center, right action will follow. This is the only true path to peace that we have. Whether we are led to make peace in our families or to work in a political peacemaking project, the right manifestation of our peacemaking can evolve only out of our own personal peace. Step together. As you do this, bring your hands to your heart center.

"Let the healing of the earth begin" is the final phrase. With this gesture imagine that you are holding the earth between your hands as gently and lovingly as possible. It is as if you were administering the "laying on of hands" to the earth herself. This is the heart of the prayer for peace in the outer world. Let your eyes follow the hands, adding as much focus and personal intention as you

can. See your own collective internal healing and see the healing of the world in turn. Hold the dream and intention together with all your heart. In this dance we are healing ourselves and healing our world. The feet step in place during this part of the dance. Repeat the sequence on alternating sides twenty to fifty times. Be at peace.

Here are the words that inspired this dance:

## "PRAYER FOR THE WARRIORS"

Om Namo Bhagavate Vasudevaya

May the warriors find peace within
And the wars of the nations end
May the warriors find peace within
Let the healing of the earth begin

With mercy and compassion, Beloved Kuan-Yin
Melt away the anger, and let me love again
Melt away this fear, and let us love again.

Om Namo Bhagavate Vasudevaya
(Thy will be done on earth as it is in heaven)

—SOPHIA

### PERSONAL EXPLORATION

The beauty of this body prayer is its two uses. One is as described earlier, a deep prayer calling for personal and collective healing. The other extraordinary use is for healing anger, rage, and exasperation—and other especially entrenched emotions.

Using this movement during these times can truly be transformative. Moving in the fisted contraction is easy when we're angry, but when we attempt to move into the openhearted gesture, it can feel as if we are cracking through plaster. The higher part of our nature is urging us to move on to forgiveness, but the rest of us is petulantly saying, "I don't think so." Herein lies the secret power of embodied prayer. Let the wisdom of the body do it for you. At first you may feel that your body cannot open in the chest or torso. The emotional armor is keeping you physically contracted. As you repeat the moving mantra of this prayer, the body will gently release the physical tension with each repetition of the movement. Soon the full range of motion will return and shortly thereafter your emotional equilibrium will be restored.

The fact that the body can be our ally in reconnecting to the higher aspects of the authentic self is probably the most important gift of our incarnation. A powerful vehicle for our spiritual journey, the body acts like a faithful horse carrying us home when we are too tired and lost to find the way back by ourselves. The beloved old friend plods on, finding the way even when we have temporarily forgotten.

Take some time now to quietly acknowledge your own body as your friend on this journey. Affirm new ways of incorporating its wisdom into the path of your own unfolding. The wisdom of the body can be the most grounded place for beginning to pick up the pieces when we are in confusion or crisis. Trust it. Treat it kindly and learn to listen to its wisdom. When faced with an important choice, notice whether each option you are considering calls forth any definable feelings in your body.

> Mine is always your Highest Thought. . . . The Highest Thought is always that thought which contains joy.
> —NEALE DONALD WALSCH,
> *CONVERSATIONS WITH GOD, BOOK 1*

## LIVE EACH DAY AS IF IT WERE YOUR LAST

The theme of the song is to hold each day—each moment—as precious, to live it as if it were your last day. How would this attitude alter your appreciation of life? I enjoy doing my stretches keeping in mind the words to the song that follows. As always, do what feels right for your own body, without stress or strain.

~

INTENTION: *As I stretch my outer being, I stretch my inner well-being, too.*
MUSIC: *"Live Each Day," by Colleen Fulmer, from the CD* Dancing Sophia's Circle, *or any other soft, relaxing instrumental music.*
EXERCISE: *Stretches.*

Before beginning the exercise, take a moment to raise your arms above your head and then to the sides of your body, to get a sense of your range of motion. Return your arms to neutral and do three winged arm stretches at shoulder level. Hands and arms begin stretched, palms down, in front of the chest. Then open them out to the sides, palms up. Repeat five to ten times.

Next, clasp your hands and press away from the chest, expanding the upper back and shoulders.

Now clasp your hands behind your back and lift them up as far as is comfortable. If this is difficult for you, try using a towel. Stretching should feel good. If it doesn't, you may be pushing too hard. Lighten up. Do only what

*Winged arm movement*

feels good in the stretch. Stretching should be pleasurable. It becomes burden-
some when you try to model someone else's flexibility that is not your own. Be
where you are. Stretch only for the pleasure it gives you.

The next sequence stretches the calf, the front of the hip, the front of the

thigh, and the back of the thigh. Facing to the right, step back with your left foot, heels to the floor, stretching your left calf. Next, bend your right knee forward, stretching the front of your left hip. Bring your hands to prayer position above your head.

Next, bend the left knee, straighten the front leg, placing the hands on the thighs for stability and support, and flatten the lower back. This stretches the hamstring (back of the thigh). Repeat on the other side.

Facing front, open in the winged movement as before, opening to wisdom, as befits the lyrics to the music.

### "LIVE EACH DAY"

You call me to walk with you
And with my words I say, "Yes!"
But you seek more than words
And my heart longs to give you more than empty promises.

*Refrain:* O to live each day as if there were no other day
To live each moment as if it were my last one
To give each breath saying yes with the whole of my life to you
This is the meaning that Wisdom has brought me to.

I've stumbled and fallen so many times,
Still you ask me to come,
For you know more than I know,
And your arms lift me up and your
Heart gives me strength to
Love again.

*Refrain*

God grant me the serenity to accept
The things I can't change,
The courage to change all that I can
And the wisdom and grace to know the difference.

*Refrain*

Each morning we greet is a gift of time,
A new beginning comes with the
Dawn: if the sun shines or in pouring rain
We can praise and thank our God
For blessings all the same.

*Refrain*

Each evening we gather remembering, all the life
That's touched us today,
And with praise on our lips as the sun goes down,
We embrace the stars of night and the blanket
Of your grace.

*Refrain*

The dreams in my heart are your presence there,
Like a full moon in the night
That sings of the love that you have for me
And in your passion deep,
There I choose to live my life.

*Refrain*

—COLLEEN FULMER

# JUST TO BE

"Just to be is a blessing. Just to live is holy. Just to be, just to live is a blessing is holy."

This meditation develops the theme that being, not only doing, is what truly defines our value as human beings. It is often only when we stop doing our daily activities that we are able to be mindful of the present moment, which holds the wonder of life and the truth of our closeness to the Holy Source of our being. This is a truly wonderful song for relaxation. Breathe it in as spiritual elixir.

Find a comfortable position and relax into the present moment, reading the following intention.

~

INTENTION: *I will remain attentive to the present this day.*
MUSIC: *"Just to Be," by Colleen Fulmer, from the CD* Dancing So-phia's Circle, *or any soft, soothing instrumental music you like.*
EXERCISE: *Relaxation/meditation.*

## "JUST TO BE"

*Refrain:* Just to be is a blessing
Just to live is holy
Just to be, just to live
Is a blessing is holy.

Be still and know I am God
In quiet and trust lies your healing
When you look you'll find me with you
When you look you'll find me with you.

*Refrain*

So beautiful wildflowers grow
They don't spin, toil or weave,
Yet their smile delights our God
Yet their smile delights our God.

*Refrain*

See all the birds of the sky
They don't gather into barns
Yet our God cares for them
Yet our God cares for them.

*Refrain*

Asleep on her mother's breast
The child is content and weaned
O my soul, trust in our God
O my soul, trust in our God.

*Refrain*

The wonder of mountains and hills
They don't worry or fret
Yet they stand, upheld by God
Yet they stand, upheld by God.

*Refrain*

Look at the rivers and seas
They run and play before God
Yet their sparkle gives our God glory
Yet their sparkle gives our God glory.

*Refrain*

Come to me all you who labor
To bring new life to the world
Lay down your cares, I will refresh you
Lay down your cares, I will refresh you.

*Refrain*

—COLLEEN FULMER

# Chapter 8

# DANCING THE ORIGINAL LORD'S PRAYER

A mystic is one whose heart, mind, and body are directly experiencing the Oneness of the Holy Source. He or she commonly feels a communion beyond words. Some have called it the Experience of Truth, others Divine Cosmic Love, still others the Great Emptiness. Jesus, Buddha, Hildegard von Bingen, Moses, Julian of Norwich, Rumi, and Saint Teresa of Avila all experienced mystic clarity. For most people, however, divine illumination evaporates quickly, and the feeling of ecstatic wonder is replaced with yearning for permanent union. In her book *Walking to Mercury*, Starhawk says, "What's important is your attempt to touch truth, not your failure to hold it."

To touch the soul of the mystic, we will use one of the most famous of Western prayers—the Our Father, or Lord's Prayer. I find that embodying this prayer awakens my ears and eyes to the deep truth of Jesus' words and to their profound mystic nature, which has been lost through successive translations of biblical scripture.

Jesus spoke Aramaic, in his day the common language of the people in that part of the world. It is a rich language with many nuances in which a single word or phrase may have as many as five to eight different meanings. Translators, who naturally work from their own cultural bias, are obliged to pick a single "best fit" for words. This can pose a problem when the source language (in this case, Aramaic) is distinctly richer in meaning than the destination language (in this case, Greek, Hebrew, Latin, or eventually English).

The many years that passed between Jesus' actual teachings and the time they were finally captured on the written page create an additional problem in understanding his original words. His teachings went from his original Aramaic to Greek to Hebrew to Latin and finally to the English version many of us have heard since our youth. Each ensuing translation stripped away a little more of the mystical content to fit not only the constraints of the language at hand but also the political and cultural agenda of the translator.

Scholar Neil Douglas-Klotz has gone back to the original Aramaic and offers us a unique look at the possibilities of meaning contained within the original Lord's Prayer. I have used his book *Prayers of the Cosmos* as the text for this program. As you will see, these translations offer a glimpse into the mind of a desert mystic whose original teachings speak to us today in ways that are relevant to all seekers of the truth, be they Christian or not. We find a Jesus who holds an open, nonsexist view of the Divine. His concept of heaven is more akin to a state of consciousness than to a nebulous place that is elsewhere. His call to the Divine carries some of the same vibrational qualities as chanting the sound of Aum (Om). This exploration of the prayer of Jesus opens the heart to the possibility of mystical communion with the Source of Oneness. These renditions of Jesus' words and the accompanying body prayers call to the hearts of all who dance with the intent of reaching the presence of the Beloved. Come to communion in a way made new.

*Note:* In a departure from the other chapters in part II, I will not give you a specific intention to remember when you learn each movement. Instead, select a phrase from the Aramaic translations listed for each line of the prayer, thereby choosing the intention that speaks to you on any given day. The approximate pronunciation is indicated after each Aramaic phrase.

# ABWOON D'BWASHMAYA

## (Birther of the Cosmos)

*Approximate Pronunciation:* ab•vwoon deb•wash•mai•ya

The Lord's Prayer is far less gendered in the original Aramaic than in the English King James Version. The word *Abwoon* is a call to the One that is neither male nor female, to the One Creative Source who gave birth to the Cosmos.

This phrase expresses deep gratitude for Divine Creation and for the Unity of all life and matter. *Abwoon* has very ancient roots. Some people believe that it is connected to the ancient Sanskrit sound of *Aum (Om)*, believed to reflect the sound of Creation itself. *Abwoon* is itself a chant. Those of you who are accustomed to chanting will notice the cranial vibration *nnn* at the end of both *Abwoon* and *Aum*. This vibration is said to represent the breath from the Oneness as it penetrates our earthly form.

The rest of the phrase has to do with the light, sound, vibration, sign, or word by which we attempt to recognize the unknowable. It is the rising and shining of Creation. It is the Universe itself. It is the Aramaic concept of heaven, existing within us and throughout the Cosmos. The idea that heaven is a place elsewhere arose from later Greek influence. The Aramaic interpretation depends more on our individual state of consciousness and the manner in which we perceive the Oneness in the Universe.

INTENTION: *Choose from the Aramaic translations.*
MUSIC: *"Shimmers in the Sand," by Phil Thornton and Hossam Ramzy, from the CD* Eternal Egypt, *or any free-flowing, evocative, exotic music. I prefer to use Middle Eastern—inspired music for this series of dances because it helps put me in the mind-set of the sound environment and culture in which Jesus lived and flourished.*
EXERCISE: *Warm-up.*

We begin this moving prayer by slowly warming up our bodies with movements that express our appreciation of Creation. Standing with your feet about shoulder-width apart, circle your arms five to eight times. Next, touch

your heart with both hands and open your arms out to either side. Touch your heart again and open to the left. Repeat and open to the right. This movement acknowledges that Spirit is within us and all around us in the Universe.

Next, we borrow a gesture from a Hawaiian tradition. Begin to step side to side. Bring one hand to the side of your mouth as if you were about to call out. Your other hand extends away from the mouth, symbolizing a voice calling out. We call to Spirit to infuse our dance. By whatever name or image we use, we call to the Great Unity, the Source of our being. Repeat this ten to fifteen times.

Next, face to your left. Step your right leg behind, bringing your heel to the floor, stretching the calf. Bring your hands out to the sides at your shoulder level. Hold for six to ten seconds. Then bend your right knee and keep your left leg straight while you bring your hands together in prayer position above your head. Next, bend your back knee, straighten the front, and flatten your lower back. You will feel this stretch in the back of the thigh. If you feel balanced enough, hold the stretch while reaching forward with the hands in a circular motion, bringing them in toward the torso and out again. The hands are making a great wheel. With this movement we acknowledge that we are part of the sacred circle, the great wheel of life. We are part of the wheel of Creation made manifest through us.

Turn toward the other direction and repeat the sequence. Come to conclusion in brief stillness, acknowledging your connection to the Oneness.

## SAMPLE TRANSLATIONS FROM *PRAYERS OF THE COSMOS*

- Birther! Father-Mother of the Cosmos, you create all that moves in light.

- Thou! The Breathing Life of all, Creator of the Shimmering Sound that touches us.

- Source of Sound: in the roar and the whisper, in the breeze and the whirlwind, we hear your Name.

- Radiant One: you shine within us, outside us, even darkness shines when we remember.

### PERSONAL EXPLORATION

The word *Abwoon* can be used as a chant by itself or with the gestures we are about to offer. The first part of the word begins with an open vowel sound, *Ah.* As you begin this part of the chant, open the arms and chest as you open your heart to the magnificence of Creation.

The *vwoo* sound is related to the sound of the breath of Spirit as it infuses all beings with life. Our own breathing becomes unified with the One Holy Breath as we consciously link with it. The hands come together above the head and begin to move down toward the head, as we sense the breath of Spirit enter our being.

The *nnn* sound creates an internal vibration in our head as we sing it. This reflects the penetration of Spirit into matter, into our being. The hands continue to move down and fold over the heart, creating an awareness of Spirit infusing us in mind and body.

# NETHQADASH SHMAKH

## (Focus Your Light within Us)

*Approximate Pronunciation:* ne•kah•deesh shuh•maak

In the Aramaic sense, a thing is made holy by setting it apart. This is akin to the creation of a separate place or room in our house in which we pray and meditate. This is both an inner and an outer experience. When we give ourselves discrete time to be in stillness, we allow the light of what is holy to live within us. The meaning is similar to the injunction "Enter into thy closet." We must first release the clutter of chattering thoughts and obsessive busyness. "Be still and know that I am God." This is done so the light of *Abwoon*, the Great Unity, may be focused within us and thus be released for use in the world.

~

INTENTION: *Choose from the Aramaic translations.*
MUSIC: *"The Land of the Pharaohs," by Phil Thornton and Hossam Ramzy, from the CD* Eternal Egypt, *or other rhythmic Middle Eastern or Indian music.*
EXERCISE: *Aerobic.*

We begin the movement in this dance by using an African gesture of sweeping the space clean. We sweep the space as we sweep and cleanse our thoughts, readying ourselves to receive the Light of Unity. Make a turn for a count of eight, sweeping with your right hand at your wrist as you turn clockwise while pulsing your chest.

Return to starting position, then reverse the motion and move counterclockwise for another count of eight. Sweep backward with your left hand, pulsing the chest and heart, "opening the heart" with the movement.

This is followed by eight side-to-side steps. With one hand to your ear, let your other hand travel away from your ear as if listening for the sound of the "still, small voice." This gesture comes from a Hawaiian dance, as did the preceding call to Spirit. Repeat this eight to ten times.

This is followed by four lunges to the front. If you are a novice or are un-certain of your knees, you may prefer to step back slightly. If you are lunging back, be sure to step back far enough to place your forward knee over the heel of the same foot. This minimizes stress to the knees. The hands here gather light from the space above the head and focus it inward. This gesture embraces the translation "Focus your light within us—make it useful." Repeat this on al-ternating legs for eight repetitions. Then turn the lunges to alternating sides for eight more repetitions as you continue this invocation. Pull all three steps to-gether for about three to six minutes, depending on your comfort level. End this exercise by bringing your feet together with your hands near the sides of your head, focusing spiritual energy within yourself. Take two deep breaths be-fore moving on.

What follows is a sampling of the possible translations for this phrase. Hold the ideas that speak to your inner being while you experiment with this series of movements.

### SAMPLE TRANSLATIONS FROM *PRAYERS OF THE COSMOS*

• Focus your light within us—make it useful: as the rays of a beacon show the way.

• Help us breathe one holy breath feeling only you—this creates a shrine inside, in wholeness.

• Help us let go, clear the space inside of busy forgetfulness: so the Name comes to live.

• Hear the one Sound that created all others, in this way the Name is hallowed in silence.

## PERSONAL EXPLORATION

Go inside yourself and breathe deeply. Notice what thoughts need to be released as you prepare to enter the sacred space of your heart center.

As you enter the stillness, let each breath release you into the Light of Spirit, as if you were letting yourself fall back into the arms of a loved one. Affirm this mantra: "I rest in love." Stay in this place of sacred rest as long as you like.

Ask the Divine Source whether there are places, things, or people that clutter this sacred space in your day-to-day life. If there is a need to release something, ask for the guidance to keep your sacred center uncluttered and the grace to release gently what is in the way of the Divine Light. Inhale and exhale three times deeply, then slowly come back from this meditation when you are ready.

# TEYTEY MALKUTHAKH

## (Create Your Reign of Unity Now)

*Approximate Pronunciation:* tay•tay mal•ku•taak

*Nethqadash shmakh* prepares a holy space inside us. *Teytey malkuthakh* offers this space as a place "to envision and prepare for new creation," one of the translations suggested by Neil Douglas-Klotz in *Prayers of the Cosmos.*

He also translates the word *malkuthakh* as projecting an image of a "fruitful arm poised to create, or a coiled spring that is ready to unwind with all the verdant potential of the earth." There is a sense of matching our individual affirmation, "I can," with the action of Divine Creation. We affirm our willingness to take a new direction in alignment with Divine Intention. Let our "I can" be united with the Oneness that Jesus called *Alaha.* We ask that our personal and collective goals be united "toward unity and creativity, like the earth's."

~

INTENTION: *Choose from the Aramaic translations.*
MUSIC: *"Isis Unveiled," by Phil Thornton and Hossam Ramzy, from the* CD Eternal Egypt, *or any music with Middle Eastern rhythms.*
EXERCISE: *Aerobic.*

The movement of *Teytey malkuthakh* begins with a box step. Cross your right foot in front of your left, then cross your left in front of your right. Step back with the right foot to the starting position, then move the left foot back to

its starting position. The arms and hands are open wide. The shoulders are loose, shimmying slightly from side to side with the rhythm, holding the intention of gathering divine purpose.

Next, step forward with your right foot, then step back for two repetitions (mambo). The hands spread our intention around us onto the earth, matching our "I can" with that of the Great Unity.

This is the moving mantra in its entirety. After twenty to thirty repetitions, change the lead leg and continue the movement, bringing balance to the prayer.

### SAMPLE TRANSLATIONS FROM *PRAYERS OF THE COSMOS*

- Create your reign of unity now—through our fiery hearts and willing hands.

- Let your counsel rule our lives, clearing our intention for cocreation.

- Your rule springs into existence as our arms reach out to embrace all creation.

- From this divine union, let us birth new images for a New World of peace.

## PERSONAL EXPLORATION

With eyes closed, stand in neutral position. Place your hands on your belly and breathe deeply, imagining that you are breathing with the rhythm of the Holy Source, expanding and contracting. With each inhalation feel the chest and abdomen expand more and more, feeling the heart center open. Walk slowly around the room, as if you were being led by your heart center. How does this alter your sense of movement? As you walk, let your arms and torso move in response to the cues your heart gives them. Sense your own "I can." Affirm: "Let the Great Unity be manifested through me now."

# NEHWEY TZEVYANACH AYKANNA D'BWASHMAYA APH B'ARHA

## (Help Us Love beyond Our Ideals and Sprout Acts of Compassion)

*Approximate Pronunciation:* neck•way tsev•ya•nak eye•kah•na deb•wash•mai•ya aaf buh•ar•hah

This next line of the prayer moves us into acts of creation in concert with the Divine Source. We are ready to put spirit into action. This part of the prayer leads us "to take responsibility for our actions and the way they affect our surroundings. To reach fulfillment, creativity must take into account the well-being of the community and of the earth" *(Prayers of the Cosmos)*.

Douglas-Klotz teaches that the concept of an otherworldly heaven is Greek. The Aramaic idea of heaven reflects Eastern philosophy and is more akin to a state of consciousness aligned with the Holy Source in the present moment. During a workshop I took from Neil, he referenced the Tibetan paintings that depict the levels of heaven (states of consciousness) above and around the head of an enlightened individual.

Many Far Eastern ideas were circulating in the Middle East during the time of Jesus, and there is speculation that he himself may have spent a number of years in India. Consider the Sanskrit chant "Om Namo Bhagavate Vasudevaya," which antedates the Lord's Prayer by centuries. It seems more than coincidence that it, too, translates as, "Thy will be done on earth as it is in heaven." This is the chant you heard in the "Prayer for the Warriors" in the preceding chapter.

INTENTION: *Choose from the Aramaic translations.*
MUSIC: *"The Cobra's Dance," by Phil Thornton and Hossam Ramzy, from the CD* Eternal Egypt, *or other Middle Eastern or rhythmic New Age music.*
EXERCISE: *Aerobic.*

The step in this embodied prayer looks Egyptian in the way that the hands are positioned. Begin in neutral position. Turn and step to your right leading with your right foot, then left and right again. On the fourth beat, begin to turn and face to your left. Step to your left now leading with your left foot. The rhythm is one, two, three, "and." The "and" (fourth beat) is where you turn your body to face the opposite direction. You move to one side and then to the other. Right, left, right moving to the right. Then turn to the left and step left, right, left. The lead hand is up with palm open, receiving inspiration and guidance. Your eyes are on the open palm to intensify intention and focus. Repeat this movement back and forth, acknowledging that life sometimes pulls us in opposing directions.

The step changes by going into double time. This reflects our lives, too. We are often buffeted to and fro, often at a pace not of our own choosing. This

is part of learning to trust and to stretch ourselves. Sometimes meeting the tempo is the way to surrender to what we are being given to do. I am not talking about the mindless addiction to speed so characteristic of Western culture. I am talking about integrating our understanding of right action with trust in the flow of spiritual guidance.

After eight repetitions of the double-time step, ground the metaphor of your actions to the earth by waving your torso and palms in a blessing to the earth. The entire sequence is three steps back and forth to each side eight times, then double time for eight repetitions, followed by four torso/chest rolls toward the earth. Repeat the entire sequence for approximately three to six minutes or until your body begins to feel fatigued. End by bringing your feet back to neutral position while you hold your palms at waist level toward the earth in blessing.

Here are some inspirations to take into your dance.

## SAMPLE TRANSLATIONS FROM *PRAYERS OF THE COSMOS*

- Let all wills move together in your vortex, as stars and planets swirl through the sky.

- Help us love beyond our ideals and sprout acts of compassion for all creatures.

• As we find your love in ours, let heaven and nature form a new creation.

• Create in me a divine cooperation—from many selves, one voice, one action.

## PERSONAL EXPLORATION

This exercise is to be done with a partner. It is called the potter and the clay. One person is the clay, as completely passive as possible. The other person, the potter, gently and lovingly molds the clay into the image of his or her liking. Take your time with this.

Clay, notice how it feels to surrender and trust the vision that the potter has for you. Potter, notice what a delight it is to work with the refined beauty of this material. What feelings does your act of creation evoke? When you come to the natural end of the exercise, change roles and begin again.

This is an obvious metaphor for surrendering the ego's desire for control to the higher purpose of Divine Will. "Thy will be done" is often easier said than accomplished. This exercise surprises many participants. The clay finds that relaxing into the guidance of the potter is actually quite enjoyable. Resistance would take a lot more energy and not be as much fun. Many people find that being the potter gives them great pleasure. They feel a deep experience of gentle nurturing as they mold the clay into its highest and most beautiful form.

# HAWVLAN LACHMA D'SUNQANAN YAOMANA

## (Grant Us What We Need Each Day in Bread and Insight)

*Approximate Pronunciation:* hahv•laan lock•mah day•soon•kuh•naan yo•mah•nah

*Lachma* is one of the Aramaic words that are rich and varied in meaning and context. It is the word for "bread" as well as for "understanding" or "insight." Its linguistic roots go back to a root *hma*, which is derived from the Divine Feminine. This is related to vigor, warmth, passion, possibility, and generative power. This root becomes the word for "Holy Wisdom" in the Book of Proverbs and the Greek Sophia feminine wisdom tradition. *Hawvlan lachma d'sunqanan yaomana* is a request not only for bread and physical sustenance but also for wisdom and insight.

The line asks for this day's measure—no more, no less. The implication is of taking only what we need, not hoarding more than we need and not taking from the earth more than is necessary. Douglas-Klotz says, "The prayer pushes us beyond an introverted spirituality to consider everything in our dealings with others" *(Prayers of the Cosmos).*

In his workshop Douglas-Klotz uses the words and intention of the line *Hawvlan lachma d'sunqanan yaomana* to celebrate a communion service. During this ritual the participants feed each other rather than taking the elements themselves. This creates a lovely attitude of sharing and mutual nurturing in the gathered community.

⁓

INTENTION: *Choose from the Aramaic translations.*
MUSIC: *"Sandalwood and Jasmine," by Terry Oldfield, from the CD* Spirit of India, *or other evocative, rhythmic music.*
EXERCISE: *Aerobic.*

This moving mantra is an open motion of receptivity. Beginning in neutral position, feet hip-width apart, step to the right side with your right foot. This side step can become a squat if you are strong enough to sustain the motion. Your arms, hands, and chest open wide to receive. Then return your feet to starting position while passing the hands in front of your eyes, the center of vision and insight. What wisdom will you integrate today? Repeat the step to the left. If you are more advanced, you may add a cha-cha between sides. Continue to alternate sides for three to five minutes' worth of music.

Here's another gesture step I will sometimes add to this: The feet are still. Raise your right knee and raise your hand overhead, then let them drift down to the earth in reverence for its gifts (in this case, of food and nourishment). This is followed by a slight bend of the torso with two motions of your hands as if you were receiving food, perhaps picking food from a plant. Coming back to standing position, send a blessing with a torso chest wave toward the earth. Come to conclusion with the natural end of the music or when your body tells you to do so. End with a final wave of blessing to the earth in thanksgiving.

## SAMPLE TRANSLATIONS FROM *PRAYERS OF THE COSMOS*

- Grant what we need each day in bread and insight: subsistence for the call of growing life.

- Produce in us, for us, the possible: each only-human step toward home lit up.

- Generate through us the bread of life: we hold only what is asked to feed the next mouth.


### PERSONAL EXPLORATION

There is an ancient concept that food contains a wisdom of its own. The speed of the stag, the strength of the ox, and the flexibility of the wheat in the fields all invigorate us with their special kind of wisdom. By eating food, we are ingesting this wisdom. Meditate a moment before each meal to consider and give gratitude for the wisdom that is present on our plates before partaking of it. Conversely, this reflection may help us rethink dietary habits that we would like to change. We can ask ourselves, "Do I really want the kind of wisdom that is present in an Oreo cookie or a can of Coca-Cola?"


# WASHBOQLAN KHAUBAYN WAKHTAHAYN AYKANNA DAPH KHNAN SHBWOQAN L'KHAYYABAYN

## (Loose the Cords of Mistakes Binding Us as We Release the Strands We Hold of Others' Guilt)

*Approximate Pronunciation:* wash•buh•klaan hkow•bain
wahk•tuh•hain ay•kah•na daaf hkuh•nahn shwah•kuhn•ul
hkai•uh•bain

One of the translations of this phrase is "Loose the cords of mistakes binding us, as we release the strands we hold of others' guilt." Many people feel that the quintessential teaching of Christianity is that of forgiveness.

There is a sense in this line that we are to loosen that which ties us up in knots inside. Again, we find the idea of releasing and letting go. The roots of the phrase can also be translated as "returning something to its original state."

This suggests that our original state is clear and unburdened. With each breath, we can release into our deep, unburdened connection with Creation.

The word *khaubayn*, which was commonly translated in Greek as "offenses" or "debts," may also mean "hidden past," "secret debt," or "hidden, stolen property." These Greek translations reflect dualistic Greek philosophy: right/wrong, good/bad, heaven/hell. However, the original Aramaic may also mean "mistakes," "failures," "accidental offenses," or "frustrated hopes." These interpretations contain less sense of judgment.

The Aramaic conveys the sense that by releasing that which ties us up in knots, we may mend our relationships and make them whole once more.

INTENTION: *Choose from the Aramaic translations.*
MUSIC: *"Desert Rhythm," by Phil Thornton and Hossam Ramzy, from the CD* Eternal Egypt, *or other Middle Eastern or rhythmic music of your choice.*
EXERCISE: *Aerobic.*

The movement I use for this dance is borrowed from a Brazilian dance in the Candomble tradition. In it we name the thing that ties us in knots or makes us ill. Then we show what this does to us internally. Finally, we release it, all within the dance.

Begin standing with feet hip-width apart and arms hanging comfortably at your sides. Inhale and exhale three times, feeling grounded, physically and mentally. Take four steps front, pounding the right fist at waist level for the first three beats. On the fourth beat, place the fist on the part of your body that is holding or manifesting the pain of your internal knot. Where does this live in your body? In your head? Is there an upset feeling in your stomach or a tight knot in your shoulders? The fourth beat shows where the unforgiven tangles live as an energy in your body.

Then take four steps back. Here you contort your body to show the ugliness of this internal conflicted mass of blocked energy. Gnarled fingers, a hunched and twisted torso, or deep furrows of pain in your face demonstrate what an unforgiving attitude toward yourself and others does to your inner being.

The final part of the dance is the release. You affirm your belief in the release of your burden. Forgiveness is indeed possible. Turn clockwise to the count of four. Your hands sweep in front of the body, at waist level, on

the count of one, sweep behind your back on two, come again in front of your body on the count of three, and release with a quick, fluid flick of the hands above the head on four as your feet come back to starting position. It's as if the hands were sweeping clean the inner turmoil, with a prayer for your return to Unity. Repeat the sequence fifteen to forty times or until your body tells you to quit. Take a deep breath and affirm that you are free of guilt and resentment.

### SAMPLE TRANSLATIONS FROM *PRAYERS OF THE COSMOS*

- Loose the cords of mistakes binding us, as we release the strands we hold of others' guilt.

- Forgive our hidden past, the secret shames, as we consistently forgive what others hide.

- Erase the inner marks our failures make, just as we scrub our hearts of others' faults.

- Untangle the knots within so that we can mend our hearts' simple ties to others.

### PERSONAL EXPLORATION—1

Ideally, this exercise should be done outside in the wind, on a breezy bluff or rooftop. Think of what it is you would like to hold in the light of forgiveness. Face the wind with arms raised above your head, palms facing the wind. Imagine that the wind is passing through your physical body, your emotional body, and your spiritual body, taking with it all the knots of guilt and judgment, the long-held resentments, all facets of the "hidden past" that have been lodged within. Stay with the cleansing winds of Spirit for as long as you wish. Notice the sense of renewal that replaces the tangled webs of your regrets. You are made new in the freshness of forgiveness.

### PERSONAL EXPLORATION—2

Another version of the preceding exercise can be done with water. Immerse yourself under a summer waterfall or meditate beside a creek while the purity of the sound washes through you. Let the sounds and the feelings of the water bring you the sense of freedom that forgiveness brings to the soul. Even the simple ritual of a daily shower can be a powerful act of inner as well as outer cleansing. This is a baptism of forgiveness in which we are made new, returning to our natural state of unity with the Spirit that lives in all beings.

# WELA TAHLAN L'NESYUNA ELA PATZAN MIN BISHA
## (Don't Let Surface Things Delude Us)

*Approximate Pronunciation:* way•luh tok•lahn leh•nes•yu•nuh ey•luh
pot•zahn min bee•shuh

In *Prayers of the Cosmos*, Neil Douglas-Klotz indicates that this line of the prayer is the least understood and most misinterpreted. Why would God lead us into temptation anyway?

Possible translations of the first part of the Aramaic line are closer to: "Don't let us be deluded by surface things that divert us from our spiritual path," or "Keep us from the inner vacillation caused by the distractions of being too busy to hear the still, small voice within." Another possibility is: "Don't let us be distracted by the illusions of materialism." Any of these interpretations make this line a lot more relevant to the world today.

The word *bisha* was interpreted by the Greeks as "evil." The Aramaic sense is closer to "error." It includes a sense of unripeness or inappropriate action. Let us do the right action at the right time. Let us not miss the opportunity for right action. It also has to do with being present so that we can know when the moment to act is at hand. Don't let us get so caught up in the big picture of our ideals that we miss the next footstep, which holds the right action to be taken. The next right action may not necessarily be to heal world hunger, a task that may feel overwhelming. It may be simply to share your lunch with a coworker who's forgotten his today.

A sense of joy is also present in this part of the prayer, as we pass on our way in freedom. We were freed by the grace of forgiveness in the preceding line. We now affirm our commitment to travel the spiritual path unencumbered by life's surface illusions.

~

INTENTION: *Choose from the Aramaic translations.*
MUSIC: *"Through the Ankh," by Phil Thornton and Hossam Ramzy, from the CD* Eternal Egypt, *or other evocative, free-flowing, rhythmic music.*
EXERCISE: *Cooldown.*

The first gesture removes the veils of illusion, pulling them aside and releasing them. This part of the dance begins from a neutral position. Step your

right foot behind your left, then step your right foot out to the side. As you step behind with the right foot, the right hand passes in front of the eyes, then moves out to the side as the right foot steps to the side. The gesture mimics removing a veil from before your eyes. Alternate sides for eight repetitions.

The next movement has the feel of grounded tai chi movements. It signifies pushing away those diversions that keep us from our true spiritual path. In the next step, lift your right knee. The left foot stays in place. Push your right hand down and away following the line of your right leg. Reverse and do the same movement on the other side. Then do eight repetitions on alternating sides.

The final step conveys a sense of uplifted joy as we savor the freedom of

the soul on its journey home. From neutral position facing front, lift alternating knees eight times. Keep your chest and shoulders lifted. Your hands are out-stretched embracing joy and freedom. Repeat this sequence of steps for three to six minutes. Feel free to end sooner or simply walk around the room to be sure that your heart rate slows down comfortably with this cooldown.

Here are some sample translations of this portion of prayer that may be useful to inspire your dance.

### SAMPLE TRANSLATIONS FROM *PRAYERS OF THE COSMOS*

- Don't let surface things delude us, but free us from what holds us back (from our true purpose).

- Don't let us enter forgetfulness, the temptation of false appearances.

- Deceived neither by the outer nor the inner—free us to walk your path with joy.

- Keep us from hoarding false wealth, and from the inner shame of help not given in time.

### PERSONAL EXPLORATION—1

The first part of this exercise helps us understand to what degree everyday "busyness" may be distracting us from deep spirituality. Sit in a meditative position in front of your television set and turn it on, preferably to a news channel with frequent commercials. Turn the volume up so that it's just uncomfortably loud. Keep the remote lying in your lap. Watch the TV and spend about thirty seconds thinking about all the things you have to get done today. Remind yourself of all the time you're wasting sitting here right now when you could be working on your "to do" list instead. Now keep your eyes open and meditate. Attempt to let your mind focus on the space between your thoughts.

After two minutes of this, point the remote at the TV and click the "off" button. Relax, close your eyes, and listen to the silence. Notice how comfortable you suddenly feel. Allow yourself to meditate comfortably for as long as you like.

When you return, remind yourself that you have a choice about the distractions you present to your mind.

### PERSONAL EXPLORATION—2

Another exploration teaches us to remain in a peaceful state regardless of the distractions around us. Again, drift into a meditative position in front of the TV. Turn it on and set the volume very low, so that you can barely hear it if you listen closely. Continue to meditate, paying no attention to the sound of the TV. Return to your surroundings every few minutes and increase the volume of the TV slightly, meditating again. When you reach a volume that prevents you from achieving a state of deep meditation, decrease the volume again and return to your inner state. Then stop for today. Tomorrow, practice this exercise again. You'll find that gradually you'll be able to experience the mindfulness of a meditative state in spite of the distraction of the television. This practice will develop your ability to shut out intrusions that interrupt your equanimity during the day. You can learn to maintain a peaceful inner center regardless of the "Sturm und Drang" of life that surrounds you.

## METOL DILAKHIE MALKUTHA WAHAYLA WATESHBUKHTA L'AHLAM ALMIN. AMEYN

### (Power to These Statements. May They Be the Ground from Which My Actions Grow. Amen.)

*Approximate Pronunciation:* meh•tool duh•lah•hkuh mahl•koo•tah wuh•hai•luh wuh•tesh•buhk•tah luh•lahm ahl•meen ah•mayn

There is controversy over whether this line of the prayer was actually part of the original prayer of Jesus. If it was not, then one very much like it would probably have been said, in keeping with the Jewish tradition of the times.

The root of the word for "kingdom," *dilakhie*, includes the idea of a fertile field from which all things can be produced. *Malkutha* reminds us again of the pregnant potential inherent in the Divine Source. *Hayla* is the word for "power," which without arrogance permeates and sustains growth. Again, we see a maternal image of God. Andrew Harvey, in his tape series *The Son of Man*, suggests that these were radical feminist concepts for the times in which Jesus lived.

*Teshbukhta,* according to Douglas-Klotz, "may be translated as 'glory' but calls forth more exactly the image of a 'song'—a glorious harmony returning divine light and sound to matter in equilibrium."

"Forever" is too abstract a translation of *l'ahlam almin*, considering the Aramaic mind-set. This is most probably another Greek influence. *L'ahlam almin* more closely means "from age to age" or "from gathering to gathering." There is a sense of the cycles of life in this phrase, in keeping with the cycles of nature as a marker of time.

The word *amen* in the Middle East was a way to affirm agreements. Its utterance was taken every bit as seriously as signing one's name to an agreement today. The older roots of *ameyn* present an image of the earth, or the ground of being from which the future will develop.

⁓

INTENTION: *Choose from the Aramaic translations.*
MUSIC: *"The Hero's Journey," by Russell Paul, from the CD* Spirit Bridges, *or any free-flowing, relaxing music.*
EXERCISE: *Stretches.*

The movement in this last phrase repeats the appreciation of Creation as a unifying outpouring of cosmic affection and love. This movement will also be the final stretching segment. We begin by lifting the arms and hands in receptivity to the Great Unity.

Keep your knees slightly bent. From here begin to circle your arms up through the ends of your fingertips as if you were drawing circles on the ceiling. Begin to lower your arms while you continue to circle your arms and hands

with palms down. Now place your hands on your thighs. Support the weight of the torso with your hands while your lower back contracts and releases four times.

Next, turn to your left. Your left leg is in front. Your right foot is behind with heel to the floor. Hold for six to ten seconds. Next, bend your front knee while bringing your hands to prayer position overhead. Breathe. Then bring your hands to the front of your thigh, bend your right knee, and straighten your left. Flatten your lower back. You should feel this stretch in the back of the hamstring (back of the left thigh). If you have the strength and balance, begin to rotate your hands in a circle over your front leg like a wheel. Imagine the wheel of life of which you are a part. Imagine the depth of this entire prayer as you have danced it today, as part of this great wheel of spiritual awakening.

Repeat on the other side. Bend both knees. Come around facing front.

Reach once more to Spirit, bring your hands to prayer position above your head, and slowly bring them down to the level of your heart, bringing the Unity into your heart. Hold and take three deep breaths. *L'ahlam almin. Ameyn.*

### SAMPLE TRANSLATIONS FROM *PRAYERS OF THE COSMOS*

- To you belongs each fertile function: ideals, energy, glorious harmony— during every cosmic cycle.

- Out of you, the vital force producing and sustaining all life, every virtue.

- Truly power to these statements. May they be the ground from which all my actions grow: sealed in trust and faith.

### PERSONAL EXPLORATION—1

Develop your own Lord's Prayer by taking your personal favorite translation of each line of the prayer from the ones offered throughout this chapter.

### PERSONAL EXPLORATION—2

As you consider each line of the prayer, develop movements that reflect your meditations. Stay with each line as long as you wish.

Abwoon d'bwashmaya
Nethqadash shmakh
Teytey malkuthakh
Nehwey tzevyanach aykanna d'bwashmaya aph b'arha
Hawvlan lachma d'sunqanan yaomana
Washboqlan khaubayn wakhtahayn aykanna daph khnan shbwoqan
 l'khayyabayn
Wela tahlan l'nesyuna Ela patzan min bisha
Metol dilakhie malkutha wahayla wateshbukhta l'ahlam almin.
 Ameyn.
L'ahlam almin. Ameyn.
L'ahlam almin. Ameyn.

# In Closing . . .

I hope this book has stimulated your own exploration of the body as a vehicle for achieving profound spiritual focus. Though we are all dancers in spirit, you do not have to be formally trained to awaken spiritual energy within you. Life is energy in motion that we share with every atom of Creation. We celebrate our moment in the sea of time by embracing our physicality with passion and gratitude.

A rabbi friend told me the following story. The rabbi's father was also a rabbi, a man of great learning and piety. He prayed, meditated, studied, and performed acts of compassion and social justice every day of his life. When the father was on his deathbed, his son asked him whether there was anything more he would have included in his spiritual journey. The old man sighed. "I wish I had gotten more in touch with the spiritual wisdom of my body." His voice became a whisper. "It was speaking to me in so many ways that I never heard."

The dance of life is performed in a circle. Let's end our explorations here the way we began them:

It is my fondest hope that you will continue in this exploration of the body at prayer on your own. Inasmuch as we teach what we need most to learn, I take no greater joy than learning from those of you who are continuing your own explorations. I would love to hear from you. Please write to me at: Spectrum Communications, P.O. Box 662, Orofino, Idaho 83544; or E-mail ilamberti@clearwater.net.

*We bring the fullness
of our attention . . .*

*. . . to a single point
of attention . . .*

*. . . within the heart.*

*May all the actions that my hands touch
this day come from this point of attention,
a reflection of spirit in action.*

To be placed on our mailing list for future workshop information and new programs as they are produced, or to order *The Aerobic Prayer Series* of videos, contact us at the above postal or E-mail address or call (800) DANCE-61 ([800] 326-2361).

I extend to you many blessings on your dancing spirit!

# BIBLIOGRAPHY

Adams, Doug. *Congregational Dancing in Christian Worship.* Richmond, Calif.: The Sharing Company, 1971.

Adams, Doug, and Diane Cappadona. *Dance as Religious Studies.* Richmond, Calif.: The Sharing Company, 1993.

Asante, Kariamu Weish, ed. *African Dance: An Artistic, Historical and Philosophical Inquiry.* Trenton, N.J.: Africa World Press, 1994.

Borysenko, Joan. *Minding the Body, Mending the Mind.* New York: Bantam, 1987.

Capoeira, Roda. "Capoeira." www.bnbcomp.net/capoeira/cap1.htm (accessed September 8, 1998).

De Sola, Carla. *The Spirit Moves: A Handbook of Dance and Prayer,* Doug Adams, ed. Richmond, Calif.: The Sharing Company, 1977.

Douglas-Klotz, Neil. *Desert Wisdom: Sacred Middle Eastern Writings from the Goddess through the Sufis.* San Francisco: HarperSanFrancisco, 1995.

———. *Prayers of the Cosmos: Meditation on the Aramaic Words of Jesus.* San Francisco: HarperSanFrancisco, 1990. Author's Web site: www.abwoon.com

Evans, Nicholas. *The Loop.* New York: Dell Publishing, 1998.

Fox, Matthew. *Original Blessing: A Primer in Creation Spirituality: Presented in Four Paths, Twenty-six Themes, and Two Questions.* Santa Fe, N. Mex.: Bear & Company, 1983.

———. *The Reinvention of Work.* New York: HarperCollins, 1994.

Hanh, Thich Nhat. *Being Peace.* Berkeley, Calif.: Parallax Press, 1987.

Harvey, Andrew. *The Son of Man*. Tape series. Boulder, Colo.: Sounds True, 1998.

*Into the Circle: An Introduction to Native American Powwows*. Full Circle Communications, 1131 S. College Ave., Tulsa, OK 74104.

"Macumba." *Britannica Online*. www.eb.com:180/cgi-bin/g?DocF=micro/365/68.html (accessed September 5, 1998).

Maltz, Maxwell. *Psycho-Cybernetics*. New York: Pocket Books, 1960.

Mbiti, John S. *Introduction to African Religion*. 2d ed. Jordan Hill, Oxford, U.K.: Heinemann Educational Publishers, 1991.

Miller, Kamae A. *Wisdom Comes Dancing: Selected Writings of Ruth St. Denis on Dance, Spirituality, and the Body*. Seattle, Wash.: Peace Works, 1997.

*The New Jerusalem Bible*. Garden City, N.Y.: Doubleday, 1966.

Nisker, Wes. *Buddha's Nature*. New York: Bantam, 1998.

Roberts, Elizabeth, and Elias Amidon, eds. *Life Prayers*. San Francisco: HarperSanFrancisco, 1991.

———. *Earth Prayers from around the World*. San Francisco: HarperSanFrancisco, 1991.

Rossi, Ernest Lawrence. *The Psychobiology of Mind-Body Healing*. New York and London: Norton, 1996.

Roth, Gabrielle. *Sweat Your Prayers: Movement as Spiritual Practice*. New York: Tarcher/Putnam, 1997.

Roth, Gabrielle, with John Loudon. *Maps to Ecstasy: Teachings of an Urban Shaman*. San Rafael, Calif.: New World Library, 1989.

Rumi. *The Illuminated Rumi*. Translated by Coleman Barks and Michael Green. New York: Broadway Books, 1997.

———. *The Love Poems of Rumi*. Edited by Deepak Chopra. New York: Harmony Books, 1998.

Sams, Jamie. *The 13 Original Clan Mothers*. San Francisco: HarperSanFrancisco, 1993.

Schroeder, Celeste Snowber. *Embodied Prayer: Harmonizing Body and Soul*. Liguori, Mo.: Triumph Books, 1994.

Silberling, Murray. *Dancing for Joy: A Biblical Approach to Praise and Worship*. Baltimore: Lederer Messianic Publishers, 1995.

Starhawk. *The Spiral Dance: A Rebirth of the Ancient Religion of the Great Goddess*. New York: Harper & Row, 1979.

———. *Walking to Mercury*. New York: Bantam Doubleday Dell, 1998.

Teppler, Sheri S. *Six Moon Dance*. New York: Avon Books, 1998.

Tesch, Luisa. *Carnival of the Spirit*. New York: HarperSanFrancisco, 1994.

Walsch, Neale Donald. *Conversations with God: An Uncommon Dialogue (Book 1).* New York: Putnam, 1996.

————. *Conversations with God: An Uncommon Dialogue (Book 2).* Charlottesville, Va.: Hampton Roads Publishing Company, 1997.

————. *Conversations with God: An Uncommon Dialogue (Book 3).* Charlottesville, Va.: Hampton Roads Publishing Company, 1998.

Williamson, Marianne. *A Return to Love: Reflections on the Principles of a Course in Miracles.* New York: HarperCollins, 1992.

————. *A Woman's Worth.* New York: Ballantine, 1994.

# Musical Resources

⌁

## SONGS USED IN *THE AEROBIC PRAYER* SERIES OF VIDEOS

The contributions from all the following artists are gratefully acknowledged. They provide us with a vital connection to the rhythm and spirit of the dance.

Anthony, Karl. "We Pray." From the CD *Live*. Anthony Music, P.O. Box 3064, Carlsbad, CA 92009; phone (800) 843-0165.

Astin, John. "Open Up." From the audiocassette *Into the Light*. Other CDs: *Remembrance* and *Reflections*. Golden Dawn Productions, P.O. Box 7681, Newport Beach, CA 92658.

Benjamin, Suzee Waters. "Open Up Your Heart," "Empty Bowl," and "The Waters Edge." From the CD *The Waters Edge*. To order CD copies of *The Waters Edge* contact NOMA—National Online Music Alliance, Suzee Waters Benjamin, artist, www.songs.com/suzee/; or call 1-800-BUY-MY-CD; or e-mail Watersb23@mindspring.com; or call Soulo Records, (615) 862-3170.

Brewer, Mike, and Tom Shipley. "Blessing." From the CD *Precious Stone*. Motherlode Music, 2229 Henry St., Bellingham, WA 98225; phone (360) 671-6371.

Cary, Donna Marie. "Real Love," "No Limit," "Nightmares," and "Matter of Choice." From the audiocassette *Real Love*. Real Love Music, P.O. Box 354, Owensboro, KY 42302.

Collie, Nan. "Magic." From the CD *Precious Stone*. Motherlode Music, 2229 Henry St., Bellingham, WA 98225; phone (360) 671-6371.

Fallon, Kathleen. "Hero." From the CD *Precious Stone*. Motherlode Music, 2229 Henry St., Bellingham, WA 98225; phone (360) 671-6371.

Fulmer, Colleen. "Just to Be," "I Am Enough," "Blessing the Divine Womb," "Live Each Day," and "Epiclesis." From the CD *Dancing Sophia's Circle*. Loretto Spirituality Network, 120 Gerbera St., Danville, CA 94506; phone (925) 964-1697.

Kalechstein, Scott. "Follow Your Heart." From the CD *Let There Be Light*. "From the Heart" and "Handle Yourself with Care." From the CD *Midwives of the Light*. "Closer and Closer" and "You Guide Me." From the CD *Eyes of God*. 204 N. El Camino Real, #E-220, Encinitas, CA 92024; phone (760) 753-2359.

Malach, Cathie, and Kim Rosen. "Kiss of Spirit." From the CD *Delphys: Ocean Born*. Delphys, 125 Hillside Ave., Kentfield, CA 94909; phone (415) 461-6915.

Omashar. "One Heart One Mind One Soul." From the CD *The Flower of Life*. Phone (500) 437-1863.

Ostroushko, Peter. "Miracle" and "Mandela." From the CD *Pilgrims on the Heart Road*. Red House Records, P.O. Box 4044, St. Paul, MN 55104.

Rand, Joanne. "Dream of Peace." From the CD *Joanne Rand Live*. Homefire Productions, P.O. Box 16038, Seattle, WA 98116; phone (206) 233-1309.

"Song Universal." From the CD *Song Universal*. Balance Productions, Inc., 245 E. 58th St., New York, NY 10022; phone (212) 971-1177.

Sophia. "Prayer for the Warriors." From the CD *Sophia Returns*. Hidden Waters Sound, P.O. Box 1207, Carmel Valley, CA 93924; phone (800) 659-5615.

Thornton, Phil, and Hossam Ramzy. "Isis Unveiled," "The Land of the Pharaohs," "Through the Ankh," "Shimmers in the Sand," "Desert Rhythm," and "The Cobra's Dance." From the CD *Eternal Egypt*. New World Music, 154 Betasso Rd., Boulder, CO 80302; phone (800) 771-0987.


## PERCUSSION CDs

D'Cuckoo. *D'Cuckoo, Umoja*. RGB Records, P.O. Box 31321, San Francisco, CA 94131.

Gordon, David, and Steve Gordon. *Sacred Earth Drums*. Sequoia, P.O. Box 280, Topanga, CA 90290; phone (800) 524-5513.

Hart, Mickey. *Planet Drum*. Rykodisc, Pickering Wharf, Bldg. C, Salem, MA 01970.

Hill, Ubaka. *Shape Shifters.* Ladyslipper, P.O. Box 3124, Durham, NC 27715.

Lewis, Brent. *Earth Tribe Rhythms*; *Rhythm Hunter*; *Primitive Truth.* Brent Lewis, P.O. Box 428, Joshua Tree, CA 92252; phone (619) 366-9540.

McGrath, Jim. *Percussive Environments*; *Soul Dancer.* Talking Drum Records, 1223 Wilshire Blvd., No. 503, Santa Monica, CA 90403; phone (310) 396-6941.

Roth, Gabrielle, and the Mirrors. *Tongues*; *Luna*; *Trance*; *Waves*; *Ritual*; *Bones*; *Initiation*; *Totem.* Raven Recording, P.O. Box 2034, Red Bank, NJ 07701; phone (201) 642-1979.

## MUSIC OF ASSORTED RHYTHMS AND LYRICS

Aglukark, Susan. *This Child*; *Arctic Rose.* Aglukark Entertainment, 5 Roundtree Rd., Suite 1002, Etobicoke, Ontario, Canada MGV56G; phone (416) 744-1513.

Allen, Linda. *Lay It Down—Images of the Sacred.* October Rose Productions, P.O. Box 5881, Bellingham, WA 98227; phone (360) 734-7979.

Berezan, Jennifer. *She Carries Me.* Jennifer Berezan, P.O. Box 3582, Oakland, CA 94609.

Bonnet, Alicia. *Trusting.* Dolphin Song, P.O. Box 1403, Mt. Shasta, CA 96067.

Carol, Shawna. *Goddess Chant.* Ladyslipper, P.O. Box 3124, Durham, NC 27715.

Circle of Women. *Circle of Women.* Earth Beat Music, P.O. Box 1460, Redway, CA 95560; phone (800) 346-4445.

Criss, Deb. *Heartbeat.* Deb Criss, P.O. Box 278, Asheville, NC 28802; phone (704) 251-1351.

Denean. *The Weaving.* Etherean Music, 9200 W. Cross Dr., #510, Littleton, CO 80123-2225; phone (800) 453-8437.

Edwards, Jonathan. *One Day Closer.* Rising Records, P.O. Box 268, Rockland, MA 02370; phone (313) 995-9066.

Enigma. *Enigma.* Polytrans, 14166 S.W. 139th St., Miami, FL 33186.

Gass, Robert. *O Great Spirit*; *Alleluia*; *Songs of Healing*; *Ancient Mother.* Spring Hill Music, P.O. Box 800, Boulder, CO 80306.

Glover, Sheila. *Power of the Soul.* Cloud 9 Music, P.O. Box 332, San Anselmo, CA 94979.

Hannah and Friends. *Walk with the Angels.* Hannah Music, P.O. Box 1880, Boyes Hot Springs, CA 95416; phone (707) 939-1181.

Koffler, Shelley. *I Become the Eagle.* Spotted Fawn Music, P.O. Box 493, Bearsville, NY 12409.

McKennitt, Loreena. *The Visit*; *The Mysts of Time*; *The Mask and Mirror*; *Elemental*; *Parallel Dreams*. North Star Music, 22 London St., East Greenwich, RI 02818; phone (800) 743-8994.

Noll, Shaina. *Bread for the Journey*. Singing Heart Productions, 16 Monte Alto Rd., Santa Fe, NM 87505.

Oman and Shanti. *Let Me Remember*. Dancing Wave Music; phone (800) 866-5430.

Roth, David. *Rising in Love*. Folk Era Productions, 705 S. Washington St., Naperville, IL 60540.

Roth, Gabrielle. A full catalog of evocative music for ecstatic dance. Raven Recording, P.O. Box 2034, Red Bank, NJ 07701.

Rugis, Anna. *Reconciliation: The Company of Saints and Sages*. Ruby Heart Records, 6308 Towar Ave., East Lansing, MI 48823.

Schroeder-Sheker, Therese. *Rosa Mystica*. Celestial Harmonies, P.O. Box 30122, Tucson, AZ 85751.

Shenandoah, Joanne. *Once in a Red Moon*; *Life Blood*. Canyon Records, 4143 N. Sixteenth St., Phoenix, AZ 85106.

Silver, Elaine. *Fairie Goddess*. Silver Stream Music, P.O. Box 435, Mt. Tabor, NJ 07878; phone (973) 442-1892.

Snow, Shelley. *Shamaneya*. Shamaneya Music, One Steele St., Suite 111, Burlington, VT 05401.

*Songs and Prayers from Taize*. GIA Publications, 7404 S. Mason Ave., Chicago, IL 60638.

Stanfield, Jana. *Brave Faith*. Faris Wheel Productions; phone (800) 530-5262.

Stillwater, Michael. *Arc in Time*. Inner Harmony Productions, P.O. Box 1315, Freeland, WA 98249.

Theil, Lisa. *Lady of the Lake*; *Invocation of the Graces*; *Song for My Ancestors*. Sacred Dream Productions, 6336 N. Oracle Rd., No. 326-307, Tucson, AZ 85704.

Van Cleave, Chris. *Beyond . . . See Beyond*. Chris Van Cleave Music, P.O. Box 1313, Virginia Beach, VA 23451.

von Bingen, Hildegard. *Vision*. Angel Records, 810 Seventh Ave., New York, NY 10019.

*Vox Diadema*. Real Music, 85 Liberty Ship Way, Suite 207, Sausalito, CA 94965; phone (415) 331-8278.

Williams, Ani, and Mazati Galindo. *Luna Trece*. White Wing Visions, P.O. Box 146, Yorba Linda, CA 92886-0146.

Zavada, Kathy. *Trust There Is Love*. Precious Music, P.O. Box 531, Mt. Shasta, CA 96067.

## SACRED DANCE GUILD

For information regarding the Sacred Dance Guild, visit the Web site at www.us.net/sdg or write to:

> Sacred Dance Guild
> P.O. Box 187
> Temple, NH 03084

# Video Resources

The following video resources can help you develop a vocabulary of movements and movement styles, which can help you discover your own embodied prayers.

Atea. *Belly Dance, Slow Moves.* Magical Motion Enterprises; phone (800) 995-6501.

Bergh, Maria Nhambu. *Aerobics with Soul: Kilimanjaro.* Bergh International Holdings; phone (800) 423-9685.

Fox, Molly. *Yoga Moves.* Peter Pan Industries, 88 St. Francis St., Newark, NJ 07105.

Hanh, Thich Nhat. *A Guide to Walking Meditation.* Parallax Press, P.O. Box 7355, Berkeley, CA 94707.

———. *Mindful Movements.* Sounds True Catalog; phone (800) 333-9185.

Jahnke, Roger, OMD. *The Essentials of Chi.* Gateways Media Group; phone (310) 273-9575.

Lamberti, Dr. Irene. *The Aerobic Prayer Series* (*One Spirit; Desert Mystic; Native Spirit; Dancing a Miracle; Sings My Soul*). Spectrum Publishing and Communications; phone (800) DANCE-61; Web site www.sacreddance.com.

Rosas, Debbie, and Carlos Rosas. *The NIAWAVE Videos* (*Roots; Jingo; Images; Groovin; Inside Moves*). NIAWAVE; phone (800) 762-5762.

Roth, Gabrielle. *The Wave.* Raven Recordings; phone (800) 76-RAVEN.

Wyoma. *African Healing Dance.* Sounds True Catalog; phone (800) 333-9185.

# PHOTO CREDITS
*(by page number)*

# INDEX

Page numbers in *italics* refer to illustrations.

# ABOUT THE AUTHOR

© Bob Tribble

Dr. Irene Lamberti is the producer, writer, and choreographer of *The Aerobic Prayer* series, seen nationally on public television. Her programs are based on the moving forms of meditation and prayer that exist in a variety of cultures, such as African, Haitian, Polynesian, Latin, Native American, East Indian, and others.

Dr. Lamberti has studied many indigenous forms of dance throughout her life. Her passionate interest has been in the way that dance integrates and embodies the dancer's personal sense of communion with the Divine. In her television programs, book, and videos, she encourages readers and viewers to let the body become a vehicle for prayer, exploration, meditation, and celebration.

In addition to her work as a producer, author, and teacher, Dr. Lamberti has been a practicing chiropractor for twenty-two years. This background makes her uniquely well-qualified to distill the spiritual qualities of the dances she teaches, while making them simple and safe for non-dancers to explore.

Dr. Lamberti is a member of the Sacred Dance Guild and leads retreats and seminars around the country. She splits her time between living in Idaho with her family and in San Francisco.